Governing through Expertise

Littoz-Monnet provides a fresh analysis of the enmeshment of expert knowledge with politics in global governance, through a unique investigation of bioethical expertise; an intriguing form of 'expert knowledge' which claims authority in the ethical analysis of issues that arise in relation to biomedicine, the life sciences and new fields of technological innovation. She makes the case that the mobilisation of ethics experts does not always arise from a motivation to rationalise governance. Instead, mobilising ethics experts – who are endowed with a unique double-edged authority, both 'democratic' and 'epistemic' – can help policy-makers manoeuvre policy conflicts on scientific and technological innovations and make their pro-science and innovation agendas possible. Bioethical expertise is indeed shaped in a political and iterative space between experts and those who do policy. The book reveals the mechanisms through which certain global governance narratives, as well as the types of expertise they rely on, remain stable even when they are contested.

Annabelle Littoz-Monnet is Professor in International Relations at the Graduate Institute in Geneva as well as Director of the Global Governance Centre. She has widely written on global governance, the politics of knowledge, international organisations and the concept of ethical expertise. Her previous publications include *The Politics of Expertise in International Organizations* (2017).

Governing through Expertise

The Politics of Bioethics

ANNABELLE LITTOZ-MONNET
Graduate Institute of International and Development Studies

CAMBRIDGE
UNIVERSITY PRESS

University Printing House, Cambridge CB2 8BS, United Kingdom

One Liberty Plaza, 20th Floor, New York, NY 10006, USA

477 Williamstown Road, Port Melbourne, VIC 3207, Australia

314–321, 3rd Floor, Plot 3, Splendor Forum, Jasola District Centre, New Delhi – 110025, India

79 Anson Road, #06–04/06, Singapore 079906

Cambridge University Press is part of the University of Cambridge.

It furthers the University's mission by disseminating knowledge in the pursuit of education, learning, and research at the highest international levels of excellence.

www.cambridge.org
Information on this title: www.cambridge.org/9781108843928
DOI: 10.1017/9781108921060

© Annabelle Littoz-Monnet 2020

This publication is in copyright. Subject to statutory exception and to the provisions of relevant collective licensing agreements, no reproduction of any part may take place without the written permission of Cambridge University Press.

First published 2020

A catalogue record for this publication is available from the British Library.

Library of Congress Cataloging-in-Publication Data
Names: Littoz-Monnet, Annabelle, 1977– author.
Title: Governing through expertise : the politics of bioethics / Annabelle Littoz-Monnet, Graduate Institute of International and Development Studies, Geneva.
Description: Cambridge, United Kingdom ; New York, NY : Cambridge University Press, 2021. | Includes bibliographical references and index.
Identifiers: LCCN 2020018987 (print) | LCCN 2020018988 (ebook) | ISBN 9781108843928 (hardback) | ISBN 9781108925785 (paperback) | ISBN 9781108921060 (ebook)
Subjects: LCSH: Bioethics – Government policy. | Expertise – Political aspects. | Ethics committees. | Science and state. | Specialists.
Classification: LCC QH332 .L58 2020 (print) | LCC QH332 (ebook) | DDC 174–dc23
LC record available at https://lccn.loc.gov/2020018987
LC ebook record available at https://lccn.loc.gov/2020018988

ISBN 978-1-108-84392-8 Hardback

Cambridge University Press has no responsibility for the persistence or accuracy of URLs for external or third-party internet websites referred to in this publication and does not guarantee that any content on such websites is, or will remain, accurate or appropriate.

Contents

Acknowledgements		*page* vi
List of Abbreviations		ix
1	Introduction: Governing Science and Technology	1
2	Re-conceptualising the Enmeshment of Knowledge and Politics	21
3	The Fabric of Ethics Experts: A Genealogy of (Bio)Ethical Expertise	40
4	Researching Embryonic Stem Cells: Bypassing Conflict	64
5	Manipulating Particles on a Small Scale: Checking the Rise of Conflict	82
6	Tracking People's Behaviour: From Conflict Containment to Conflict Manoeuvring	101
7	Conclusion	122
Annex European Group on Ethics Experts 1991–2020		133
Bibliography		137
Index		155

Acknowledgements

The idea for this book emerged some years ago, out of a general academic interest in the relationship between knowledge and politics, and stumbling over the concept of 'expert bioethicists' or 'ethical expertise', which I found, at least, intriguing. Was it good news that specialists were being trained to guide us in our ethical choices on life sciences, questions related to the beginning and end of life as well as new dilemmas related to scientific and technological innovation? Making an academic project out of this broad questioning was a process that took most of the past six years of my academic time. It included trials, errors, reformulations of my questions, expansion of my focus of study and re-conceptualisations of my analytical framing. This book would not have been possible without the generous support of academic funding, precious insights from interviews, and also encouragement and constructive criticism from colleagues, students, friends and family.

The book represents years of research support by the Swiss National Science Foundation (SNSF) (in particular Projects 172570 and 153197). I am indebted to the SNSF for its financial support, as well as to Clarissa Brack Burdeu and Camilla Morais Silva from the Global Governance Centre for helping me out with all the administrative matters related to the management of the projects. I am also grateful to Columbia University for hosting me during my sabbatical leave in spring 2016; this was both an enjoyable and a fruitful writing semester.

My colleagues at the Graduate Institute have provided me with encouragement and feedback throughout the writing process of the book, from probing its very idea to reading draft chapters and thinking with me about its cover picture. Their constructive and thought-provoking comments, always encouraging me to look at new facets of my object of study and think outside the box, have been valuable throughout. Special thanks go to Liliana Andonova, Tom Biersteker, Susanna Campbell, Deval Desai, Emily Meierding, Stephanie

Acknowledgements

Hofmann, Keith Krause, Anna Leander and Lisa Pruegl, who took the time to read and offer comments on some chapters, as well as Monique Beerli, Gian Luca Burci, Moira Faul, Velibor Jakovleski, Suerie Moon, Aurel Niedelberger, Nina Reiners and Amalia Ribi-Forclaz, who all attended some of my talks, gave encouragement and shared inspiring thoughts afterwards.

I am grateful to my doctoral supervisee, Juanita Uribe Garcia, who has also read early versions of the book's chapters, and was always to the point and very constructive. Thanks as well, Juanita, for going through the lengthy task of constructing the book's index. Special thanks also go to Ceren Bulduk, Tomas Garzon de la Rosa, Xinju Juan and Daniel Norfolk, who all have worked as my research assistants at different stages of the project. I am very grateful to Tomas and Daniel, who did preliminary research and literature reviews on two cases in the book. I also would like to warmly thank Ceren who both commented on my work and helped me out with the monotonous but essential task of completing and editing the book's footnotes and bibliography, as well as Xinju, for compiling my list of abbreviations and other 'prelims' content.

The diverse and bright student community at the Graduate Institute has been a great source of inspiration and motivation in general and I have greatly enjoyed my conversations with them both in class and outside.

Beyond the Graduate Institute, many colleagues and friends commented on various iterations of chapters, providing insightful comments on both the case-related material as well as the theoretical discussion. Next door at the University of Lausanne, I was delighted to have conversations on expertise and politics with a number of colleagues, who invited me to give talks on my book and engaged creatively and incisively with my work. Romain Felli, Jean-Christophe Graz, Rahel Kunz, Lucile Maertens and Yannis Papadopoulos all discussed the project in various forms and at different stages. A little further away in Switzerland, thanks go to Tina Freyburg, who gave helpful comments at a conference, as well as Frank Schimmelfennig, who gave me insightful advice when the book was still just an idea.

And of course, I have greatly benefited from exchanges with friends and colleagues during conferences and workshops in Europe and North America. Christina Boswell, Falk Daviter, David Demortain,

Peter Haas and Jason Weidner, who also explore knowledge and expertise, all shared inspiring thoughts with me. François Forêt, Philip Schlesinger and Jim Dratwa, who share my interest in Europe, values and ethics, helped me think of my object of study in that particular context.

I am of course deeply indebted to all the policy officials from the European Commission as well as members of the European Ethics Group who gave me their time and insights during interviews.

Thanks also to John Haslam from Cambridge University Press for his initial interest in my book and his excellent work in bringing this project to fruition. Almost last, but definitely not least, I would like to warmly thank the two anonymous referees who read my book so carefully and shared in-depth, incisive and constructive comments which, without any doubt, helped make the book far more compelling.

And most of all, thank you to Christoph, for listening to my endless musings about the book (and much else) with great patience. And to my children, Félix and Cléo, who 'helped' just by being their cheerful and lovely selves and keeping my mind sound by distracting me with all sorts of non-academic matters.

Abbreviations

ANEC	European Consumer Voice in Standardisation
ART	Assisted reproductive technology
BBC	The British Broadcasting Corporation
BEPA	Bureau of European Policy Advisors
BEUC	European Consumers' Organisation
CCNE	*Comité Consultatif National d'Ethique*
CEEAB	Central and East European Association of Bioethics
COMECE	Commission of the Bishops' Conferences of the European Community
CORE	Comment on Reproductive Ethics
CSEP	Centre for Social Ethics and Policy (at Manchester University)
DG	(European Commission) Directorate General
DG CONNECT	Directorate General for Communications Networks, Content and Technology
DG ENTR	Directorate General for Enterprise and Industry
DG HOME	Directorate General for Home and Migration Affairs
DG INFSO	Directorate General for Information Society and Media
DG JUSTICE	Directorate General for Justice, Fundamental Rights and Citizenship
DG RESEARCH	Directorate General for Research and Innovation
DG SANCO	Directorate General for Health and Consumers
DNA	deoxyribonucleic acid
EC	European Commission
ECJ	European Court of Justice
EDPR	(EU's) General Data Protection Regulation
EDPS	European Data Protection Supervisor
EDR	European Digital Rights
EEC	European Economic Community

EES	Entry/Exit System
EFNA	European Federation of Neurological Associations
EFPIA	European Federation of Pharmaceutical Industries and Associations
EGAN	European Genetic Alliances' Network
EGE	European Group on Ethics in Science and New Technologies
ELSA	European Ethical, Legal and Social Aspects
ENVI	European Parliament's Committee on the Environment, Public Health and Food Safety
EPDA	European Parkinson's Disease Association
EPP-ED	European People's Party–European Democrats
EPPOSI	European Platform for Patients' Organisations, Science and Industry
ERAB	European Research Advisory Board
ETC Group	Action Group on Erosion, Technology and Concentration
ETP	European Technology Platform (on Nanomedicine)
EU	European Union
FP	(European Union's) Framework Programme
FTC	Federal Trade Commission
GAEIB	Group of Advisers on the Ethical Implications of Biotechnology
GM	genetically modified
GMO	genetically modified organism
hESC	human embryonic stem cell
HIV/AIDS	human immunodeficiency virus infection and acquired immune deficiency syndrome
IBC	International Bioethics Committee
ICT	information and communication technology
IR	international relations
IRB	Institutional Review Board
IVF	in vitro fertilisation
LEDP	Law Enforcement Data Protection (Directive)
MEP	Member of the European Parliament
N&N	nanoscience and nanotechnology
NBAC	National Bioethics Advisory Commission
NEC	National Ethics Councils
NEC Forum	National Ethics Councils Forum

List of Abbreviations   xi

NEH	National Endowment for the Humanities
NGO	non-governmental organisation
NIH	National Institutes of Health
NNI	National Nanotechnology Initiative
NSA	(US) National Security Agency
PCSBI	Presidential Commission for the Study of Bioethical Issues
PGD	preimplantation genetic diagnosis
PIA	privacy impact assessment
PNR	Passenger Names Record
R&D	research and development
rDNA	recombinant DNA
REACH	Registration, Evaluation, Authorisation and Restriction of Chemicals
RTD	research, technical development, and demonstration
SCENIHR	Scientific Committee on Emerging and Newly Identified Health Risks
STS	science and technology studies
SWIFT	Society for Worldwide Interbank Financial Telecommunication
UCSF	University of California, San Francisco
UK	United Kingdom
UNESCO	United Nations Educational, Scientific and Cultural Organisation
US	United States
WHO	World Health Organization

1 Introduction: Governing Science and Technology

'First do no harm,' Greek physician Hippocrates allegedly told his fellow colleagues back in the fifth century BC. Moral questions about the ethics of medicine and related areas have been asked for as long as people have asked questions about human morality. But while responses have traditionally been given by philosophers or priests, and later on by doctors and scientists themselves, the past few decades have given rise, in pluralist democracies, to a new caste of professionals whom we might call 'expert bioethicists' or 'ethics experts'.[1] These new specialists claim expertise in the ethical analysis of issues which arise in relation to biomedicine, research and innovation in the life sciences, and increasingly so in new fields of technological innovation. They have provided policymakers[2] with advice on issues ranging from the role of humans in biomedical research, the definition of life and death, animal testing and redistributive issues with regard to health, to new

---

[1] The terms 'expert bioethicist' or 'ethics expert' will be used interchangeably in this book, as is the case when references are made to such experts in policy debates or when such experts define themselves.

[2] The term 'policymaker' refers in this book to bureaucrats or politicians alike. Bureaucrats can indeed perform policymaking roles, while politicians may want to 'technocratise' policymaking for various reasons. Political scientists have indeed questioned whether it makes sense to draw any clear distinction between politics and administration (Peters 1995). A number of scholars have argued that administrations do not simply execute policies set in place by politicians, but have various tools at their disposal to shape policy. Bureaucrats, from this perspective, are deeply involved in policymaking and fight for their own conception of 'good policies' in various ways (Peters 1987, p. 257). Beyond the well-known claim that implementation can shape policy (Pressman and Wildavsky 1973), some studies have evidenced the impact of bureaucrats at the agenda-setting stage of the policy process. Kingdon, for instance, points to their influence on the definition of alternatives, although he qualifies this impact as 'indirect' since it is mediated through political actors (Kingdon 2003, p. 32). Others have concentrated on the way bureaucrats write legislation and do policy work (Page 2003). Thus, bureaucracies can act as autonomous actors and perform policymaking roles in various ways. See, for instance, Peters 1987, p. 257 on this matter.

technologies such as synthetic biology, gene editing, or even artificial intelligence. Typically, one would not expect experts or specialists to play a central role in policy areas where politics, and values, are so explicit. The book challenges these expectations, and shows that even when questions of 'right' or 'wrong' have been central in political debates, we can observe the ubiquitous role of experts. The existence of ethics experts signals an expansion of the boundaries of expert authority over a new – and contested – ontological domain, which has to do with the ethical choices made by a given society.[3]

The book examines this phenomenon and asks how the notion of ethics expertise has emerged, how its mobilisation plays out in the governance of scientific and technological innovation and how such expertise is produced. Through a close-up of ethics expertise, it sheds new light on the role of experts in global governance more broadly and beyond the case of ethics expertise. It reveals that expertise – at least when it is mandated by policymakers – is fundamentally political in three distinct but interrelated ways.[4] First, the mobilisation of expert knowledge in policy does not always arise from a motivation to rationalise governance – the 'science speaking truth to power' image. Mobilising experts can be a way of manoeuvring through political conflicts, because the mobilisation of expertise can hide the political component of public discussions, insulate policymaking and facilitate the fabric of policy compromises. This points to the endogeneity of informal mechanisms of governance in supranational arenas. Second, expert knowledge and policy do not belong to impervious and distinct spheres; experts can be mobilised to such avail because the production of expertise does not take place independently from politics. Expertise is produced at the junction of policy and science and iterations between the two spheres take place through both diffuse and tangible mechanisms, so that expertise ultimately *makes policy possible*, rather than provide it with either guidance or oversight. Third, the delineation of what counts as expert knowledge – and of what is recognised as a field of expertise – fluctuates and results from specific political and social circumstances and the professional agendas which actors unfold in given contexts.

[3] Kelly 2003.
[4] See discussion on the scope of the argument and the specificities of mandated expertise later in this Introduction, in the section 'The Enmeshment of Expertise and Politics'.

The idea of expert knowledge in the field of ethics is a relatively recent phenomenon, testifying to the fluid boundaries dividing expert from non-expert knowledge and the contingent nature of what counts as expertise.[5] The making of expert bioethicists has taken place in a context where neither traditional moral authorities nor scientists themselves appeared any longer able to provide responses to the ethical questions that arose in the face of new scientific and technological developments. In a secular age, time for the teachings of priests, imams or rabbi seemed to have passed. At the same time, the authority of scientists to decide on their own practices was being increasingly contested. Several occurrences of blatantly unethical practices in medical research made the news in the United States in the late 1970s, revealing to the public that professional norms alone were not sufficient to regulate doctors' practices.[6] At the same time, molecular biologists discovered that they could slice and combine genetic material from multiple sources, thereby creating DNA sequences in the laboratory that do not naturally exist.[7] This breakthrough swiftly triggered a dispute amongst scientists about the risks involved in the unregulated proliferation of hybrid organisms. A decade later controversies over nuclear energy, the genetic modification of food, cloning, human embryonic stem cell (hESC) science and reproductive medicine exploded, prompting further the questioning of existing governance mechanisms for the regulation of scientific and technological innovation. The emergence of these polemics destabilised 'the symbolic framework underlying the main forms of science government, namely, scientific self-government and exclusive state-science relations'.[8] Public and academic commentators became censorious of exclusive reliance on scientific expertise as a means of escaping ordinary means of public accountability. Citizens started to require greater

---

[5] See Jasanoff 1987.
[6] A medical experiment took place between the 1950s and the 1970s at the Willowbrook facility, an institution for the people with an intellectual disability on Staten Island, where a research team fed the hepatitis virus to sixty healthy children in order to observe the course of the illness. Another experiment was conducted between the mid-1930s and the early 1970s at Tuskegee in Alabama, and consisted of leaving poor black men untreated for syphilis in order to study the effects of advanced syphilis. See Chapter 3 for a full account.
[7] DNA stands for deoxyribonucleic acid, the hereditary material in humans and almost all other organisms.
[8] Braun et al. 2010, p. 512.

participation in decision-making, both in domestic and in global governance arenas. In this context, scientific controversies were increasingly framed as moral rather than simply technical disputes, and debates began to focus not only on how science should be performed but on whether some types of scientific enquiry ought to be practised at all.[9]

In this context, ethics advisory committees have been created, both in domestic and global arenas, to provide ethical assistance on policy.[10] In what has been characterised as 'ethics creep', ethics experts are now consulted for the needs of policy at every level of governance.[11] Whereas their emergence was initially a US and then a Western European phenomenon, such groups have more recently also been created in a number of other countries, such as Mexico, Japan, Turkey, Russia and Israel, to name a few.[12] In recent years, international organisations have promoted the creation of ethics committees in Africa, Latin America and the Caribbean, and they also mobilise expert bioethicists for their own needs as they are becoming increasingly involved with the governance of scientific and technological developments.[13]

Policymakers in pluralist democracies have presented ethics committees as a novel, more diverse, more deliberative and altogether more democratic form of advisory mechanism. On the one hand, ethical

---

[9] See Nelkin 1995.
[10] Policymakers have also developed inventive mechanisms to govern science, such as 'communities of engagement', citizens' panels or other forums to engage the public in scientific issues. Such mechanisms have, however, remained occasional and 'ad hoc'.
[11] Haggerty 2004.
[12] In the United States, the first bioethics commission came in the form of an ad hoc presidential commission during Jimmy Carter's tenure between 1977 and 1981. The Clinton administration appointed the National Bioethics Advisory Commission (NBAC) in 1996, thus institutionalising a system of ethical advice that had already been in place for more than a decade. In Europe, President François Mitterrand established the first group to provide ethical assistance to policy – the *Comité Consultatif National d'Ethique* (CCNE) – in 1983. Denmark set up its own council of ethics in 1987. Other European countries followed the move, with the UK creating the Nuffield Council on Bioethics in 1991, and Belgium setting up its own commission in 1993. Germany caught up with the creation of its *Nationaler Ethikrat* in 2001 (now called *Deutscher Ethikrat*), with Austria and Switzerland creating their own bioethics councils the same year. See Chapter 3 for a more detailed overview.
[13] Littoz-Monnet 2015, 2017.

expertise does differ from traditional scientific expertise in significant ways. Ethics committees typically incorporate a greater diversity of disciplinary voices. They normally include scientists in a traditional sense – medical doctors trained in ethics, molecular biologists or neurologists who have added to their trajectory some form of training in medical ethics – but also philosophers, lawyers and on some occasions theologians. They also offer a singular type of expert advice, which aims at guiding policy on the 'right' ethical path, rather than advising specific policy choices on grounds of scientific rationality. Their guidance is not primarily concerned with facts, but with values and norms. This implies that ethics experts use different methods of work, essentially engaging with what they would themselves characterise as a systematic treatment of existing ethical positions on a given problem, in an attempt to reach a position on the 'right' approach to a particular problem. The dominant view on bioethical expertise sees it as the ability to 'apply argumentative tools to moral issues and cases'.[14] Expert bioethicists are thus expected to understand moral concepts – theories and principles of applied ethics – and moral arguments. The interdisciplinarity of ethics groups invests such experts with an aura of reflexivity, making it possible for policymakers who mobilise them to claim that they have consulted broadly and openly on the ethical implications of specific scientific and technological developments.

On the other hand, the authority of ethics experts is based on epistemic expertise or claims to special knowledge. Although this conception of expertise is contested, expert knowledge is generally understood as a form of codified knowledge, either produced by specialists, or which involves specialist or technical methods, equipment or accumulated knowledge. What qualifies individuals as specialists often relates to their institutional affiliations or qualifications. Producers of expert knowledge need to demonstrate their credentials though their belonging to an academic institution, their training, or publications and participation in conferences.[15] Although other forms of knowledge, such as professional knowledge, knowledge through experience or 'lay knowledge', are also increasingly acknowledged as valid alternative forms of knowledge,[16] knowledge based on academic specialised training still holds a privileged position. The creation of specialised academic

---

[14] Sanchini 2015, p. 55.   [15] See Boswell 2009, pp. 24–5.
[16] Leander and Waever 2018.

programmes in applied ethics and bioethics (first in the United States in the 1970s–1980s, then in Europe) has therefore played an instrumental role in establishing the notion of an autonomous field of expertise in bioethics. Ethics experts themselves take great care to present themselves as 'independent', 'objective' and 'neutral' possessors of specialist, academic knowledge. Bioethical expertise can thus be interpreted as an attempt to present moral argumentation as a rational endeavour.

Thus, despite the common portrayal of ethics advisory committees as more deliberative sites of governance, the emergence of ethics expertise bestows a specific authority in morals upon specialists who claim to be applying objective knowledge and systematic and universal tools of analysis. This of course is problematic, since every community of some form, and one might say every individual, holds some set of moral values and principles, and it is not clear how any kind of *specialists* can claim universal expertise in this area. The authority of ethics experts is thus double-edged. On the one hand, it is 'democratic' in that ethics bodies *claim* to represent a diversity of voices and moral positions, and on the other, it is epistemic, in that ethics experts act as specialists who reason 'objectively'. This gives ethics experts a unique role in the governance of scientific and technological innovation.

In exploring this phenomenon, the book asks two questions. First, to what avail do policymakers increasingly resort to a new category of expert bioethicists and how does their mobilisation play out in the governance of scientific and technological innovation? Second, how is ethics expertise – a typical example of expertise mandated by policymakers – produced and in what context had it emerged in the first place? In particular, what is the relationship between experts and policymakers in processes of knowledge production and what are the more specific iteration mechanisms between the two spheres? The following section details the book's argument.

Argument: The Politics of Bioethics

A dominant pro-science and innovation narrative informs policies on scientific and technological innovation, particularly in the West. This governance narrative, or 'sociotechnical imaginary',[17] or 'culture of action',[18] conceives biological, biomedical and scientific knowledge

[17] Jasanoff and Kim 2015.   [18] Klawiter 2008.

more generally as a key source of innovation which must not be hampered for productive and competitive ends. Scholars from different fields have well captured what they call the 'pro-innovation bias' of decision makers – the tendency of decision makers to be favourable to scientific and technological innovation, because it is associated all at the same time with progress, modernity, economic competitiveness and growth.[19] Policymakers in the West broadly adhere to this narrative, to the extent that innovation is seen as a panacea for the solving of an exponential set of problems.

The 'speed imperative' – the general push to put new products into markets as fast as possible – is embedded in this dominant narrative. Policymakers' decisions are often informed by the fear of 'lagging behind' or 'losing markets', conceiving innovation as a race or competition between firms, nations, cities or different regions of the world.[20] In its 2015 Innovation Strategy, the OECD states that 'New sources of growth are urgently needed to help the world move to a stronger, more inclusive and sustainable growth path following the financial crisis. Innovation – which involves the creation and diffusion of new products, processes and methods – can be a critical part of the solution.'[21] This pro-innovation bias is shared by regulatory experts who sit in regulatory agencies or mandated expert groups who evaluate technologies and their risks. These experts are often cognitively too close to both policymakers and the industry and sustain 'set methods and ways of (not) seeing risks' and act as 'agents of broader strategies of active production of doubt and ignorance'.[22] Economists and consultants also support such policies by producing models of innovations presented as means to guide policies.[23] Innovation is broadly understood as something desirable and measurable, and existing measurement techniques of the risks related to scientific and technological innovation are informed by or embedded into this narrative.

Decision makers are therefore particularly wary of potential conflicts related to their scientific and technological agendas. While the industry – either pharmaceutical, chemical, biotech or telecom – typically expects high financial gains from the commercialisation of new technological applications, consumers or environmental groups want to be informed

---

[19] Rogers 1983; Abrahamson 1991; Fougère and Harding 2012.
[20] Hasu et al. 2012.   [21] OECD 2015, p. 2.   [22] Demortain 2017, p. 145.
[23] Godin 2015.

about the potential hazards of scientific and technological innovations, and typically have a more cautious attitude. Controversies over nuclear energy, genetically modified organisms (GMOs), stem cells or, more recently, mobile telephony have led to public debates and the questioning of science as an emblem of modernity. Groups of activists, consumers and even scientists have voiced their concerns about the risks, but also the ethical substance, of certain scientific and technological developments. Various movements have organised themselves to challenge science and technology.[24] Religious groups, for religious ethical motives, or environmental groups, out of a concern for the protection of nature as well as human health, have been raising principled opposition to the authorisation of certain technologies or practices permitted by scientific advances.[25] In the absence of consensually accepted regulatory frameworks, as is typically the case for the regulation of new fields of scientific and technological innovation, policymaking easily lends itself to politicisation and conflict.

The book makes the case that when policymakers want to push ahead potentially controversial policy agendas but fear public opposition, the mobilisation of ethics experts can act as a mechanism of stabilisation and pre-empt, bypass or tame conflicts. While maintaining an appearance of broader consultation and dialogue, mobilising ethics experts in fact helps ensure that policy remains insulated. Because it allows policymakers to not open up bioethics deliberation to the broader public or alternative (expert) voices (while claiming to be doing just this), the mobilisation of bioethics expertise acts as a particularly effective mechanism of policy insulation. Finally, resorting to expertise can facilitate the delineating of workable policy scenarios. When actors' positions are not reconcilable, policymakers try to find alternative arenas for the delineation of acceptable solutions. In such circumstances, expert groups can be mobilised, because experts' discussions typically invest a format that focuses on the technicity of issues, leaving aside, or at least making more opaque, the more fundamental political implications at stake.[26] The authority of ethical expertise rests indeed on assumptions of rationality and objectivity. Experts, moreover, tend to internalise their role as that of technical advisors, rather than political advocates, thus facilitating more

[24] Nelkin 1995, p. 445.   [25] Steven 2009; De Vlieger and Tanasecu 2012.
[26] Robert 2010b.

consensual and less conflicting discussions.[27] The scenario delineated in the expert arena can then be presented as a legitimate end point in the political process and help unlock political debates.

The mobilisation of ethical expertise can serve such functions because mainstream bioethics is itself an expert discourse that has been shaped in a political and iterative space between experts and those who do policy, and serves well the pro-science and innovation agendas of policymakers. Although the bioethics movement arose as an alternative discourse put forth by citizens, activists and a handful of scientists concerned with the way decisions on science were being made, it has been co-opted by the creation of new specialists in the field. Bioethical expertise has been stabilised around a specific set of doctrines, essentially a utilitarian framework which acts as another assessment technique in a market economy. The content and form of ethical expertise does not contain the possibility of questioning the purpose for which we do science or develop technology. There is, thus, a dynamic of co-legitimation between bioethics and politics, but the alignment of bioethics with policymakers' pro-science and innovation agendas was one which needed to be stabilised through specific mechanisms as the policy process unfolded in given issue domains. These mechanisms, or logics of iteration between knowledge and politics, which I label 'orchestration', 'ideational alignment' and 'calibration', are introduced in the theoretical discussion in the following section. They point to the enmeshment between knowledge and politics and, more tangibly, between all the actors – experts, policymakers and private actors – who shape the way a specific issue domain is governed.

Conceptualising the Relationship between Expertise and Politics

Existing research on the role of knowledge in policy has long assumed, and often still does, that policymakers resort to expert knowledge in order to improve the quality of policy choices. This view has emerged amongst political scientists back in the 1950s, when a group of scholars developed hopes that policymakers would advance better policy agendas and programmes if they employed academic research in the formulation of their decisions. If science produces objective and 'true' knowledge, the claim was, then a better use of such knowledge in policy

[27] Abélès and Bellier 1996.

should also make for better decisions and policies.[28] This approach has stimulated an innovative research programme on the role of scientists and experts in policymaking, but has remained essentially concerned with identifying the scope conditions of the influence of expert knowledge on policy, assuming that the problem at stake is the insufficient use of academic findings by policymakers.[29] This approach ignores the way policymakers can mobilise scientific research for other purposes than that of 'knowing better'. It also does not engage with the way knowledge itself can be politicised – essentially conceiving knowledge and policy as belonging to two distinct spheres with fundamentally different logics and modes of legitimation.[30] Because of its failure to capture iterations between knowledge and politics, existing research does not bring to light the complex roles which the mobilisation of experts can in turn play in governance processes.

Scholars in science and technology studies (STS) have long pointed out, for their part, that scientific activity is 'located within academic, industrial and governmental settings'.[31] From that perspective science 'embeds and is embedded in social practices, identities, norms, conventions, discourses, instruments and institutions'.[32] Bruno Latour has argued that scientific knowledge enjoys no independence or claim to authority beyond the political and economic interests that helped develop the scientific claims.[33] Critical works point to the way knowledge is subordinated to broader social structures of control, such as capitalism or the need for centralised state control.[34] 'Co-production', a concept coined by Sheila Jasanoff, depicts the way scientific ideas and beliefs evolve together with the representations and discourses that give practical effect and meaning to ideas and objects. Knowledge and the social would, thus, be characterised by a perpetual and mutually reinforcing dynamic.[35] That knowledge is at once a product and a producer of

---

[28] Lasswell and Kaplan 1950. See also Lane 1962 and Bell 1960 for an argument on the need for rational and well-founded policy, detached from politics.
[29] See, for instance, Verdun 1999; Zito 2001; Elvins 2003; Haas and Stevens 2011.
[30] Caplan 1979. [31] Irwin et al. 1997, p. 22. [32] Jasanoff 2004, pp. 2–3.
[33] Latour 1987.
[34] See Litfin 1994; Callon et al. 2009. On the relationship between science and the state, see the seminal works of Foucault (1978) and Scott (1998).
[35] See, for instance, Jasanoff 2004. For good examples of works that have challenged the assumption of science as an autonomous sphere whose norms are constituted independently of other forms of social activity, see also Shapin and Shaffer 1985; Latour 1993.

forms of social life is difficult to deny. But the co-legitimation of knowledge and politics is not something automatic or given. The relationship between knowledge and politics is entangled, but agency, contestation and conflict remain possible. The co-legitimation of science and politics is contingent and constantly needs to be (re-)stabilised. This becomes evident when one brings the focus of analysis down to the meso-level of the governance process, where policy debates in given domains are formulated, actors talk and negotiate and policy solutions are designed.

Thinking through the lens of co-production does not really help us capture *moments of destabilisation*, when the co-legitimation dynamic between knowledge and politics breaks, and things seem to be falling apart. In these moments, new concerns emerge, and existing narratives and the governance arrangements that embody them become contested. It is during such moments that new types of knowledge may emerge, because existing governance narratives and the types of knowledge they rely on become contested. One needs to reinstate the possibility of agency and alternative ways of knowing and thinking in order to understand such moments of destabilisation.

Factors of destabilisation can be manifold. Events perceived as disruptive, scientific innovations, the publicisation of new 'facts' in the media, the activism of specific groups who bring problems to light, and the role of entrepreneurial policymakers can all contribute to the destabilisation of existing governance narratives and the forms of expertise they rely on. Bioethics emerged in such a moment of destabilisation, when the governance mode in place – scientific self-government, by which scientists defined their own norms and practices – became contested.[36] Amidst the general sense that scientists did not always behave in ethical ways in light of contemporaneous standards, existing ways of doing things had to be renegotiated. Other accounts have also revealed that new forms of knowledge emerge in such moments of destabilisation in other domains. For instance, Best discusses the emergence of provisional expertise as a response to various instances of governance failure, while Eyal describes how 'knowledge through experience' has gained ground in his study of public responses towards autism when traditional authorities became contested.[37] But what

---

[36] See Chapter 2 for a more extended definition of 'governance narratives' and 'governance modes'.
[37] Best 2014; Eyal 2013.

happens after such moments of destabilisation, and the possibility of alternative or dissident knowledge actually replacing old orders, is also constrained by hierarchies and the distribution of resources.

Conversely, co-production does not address the question of how specific governance narratives and the kinds of expertise they rely on remain stable despite the presence of (explicit, implicit or potential) conflicts at the meso-level of the policy process. Even during seemingly stable periods of time, dominant narratives and the forms of knowledge they rely on can be contested by citizens, activists or 'dissident' expert voices. Policy controversies often arise in relation to scientific and technological innovation. Yet, policymakers and experts seem to be sharing specific ways of knowing, selecting and tackling policy problems that resist such contestation, whether in domains related to science and technology policy, at stake here, finance, security or agriculture. But this ideational alignment between those who decide and those who advise is stabilised in an iterative space in which experts and policymakers interact in various ways.

The book brings to light three core logics of iteration between experts and policymakers, which I label 'orchestration', 'ideational alignment' and 'calibration', and which act as *stabilisation mechanisms*. Looking at the relationship between knowledge and politics through the lens of these three concepts allows us to go beyond the somehow abstract nature of co-production, which while central to our understanding of co-legitimation processes between national narratives and certain knowledge forms at a macro-level of analysis, does not identify the mechanisms that stabilise the relationship between knowledge and politics at the meso-level of governance processes despite phenomena of agency, conflict and contestation. I argue, first, that processes of knowledge production can be orchestrated, either by policymakers or by other governance actors who have the resources to do so in a given domain. Policymakers can, for instance, frame experts' discussions. They can do this by asking experts specific questions, thus delineating the scope of their possible proposals, or by providing them with evidence on the policy process, the contours of the policy debate and the issue at stake itself, in an attempt to directly influence their thinking. This is an efficient mechanism of stabilisation which diminishes the possibility of dissenting voices and alternative modes of thinking amongst experts. Private actors through their financial or epistemic resources can also orchestrate debates through the funding of research or active lobbying strategies. The logic of orchestration is key, because it allows us to take into account hierarchies and unequal resources and how this may affect which discourses and forms of knowledge become dominant.

The unilaterality of this logic, however, is diluted throughout the policy process, because other mechanisms are at play. Experts' ways of thinking may indeed be *ideationally aligned* with dominant policy narratives. It is the participation of experts, policymakers and other actors (private actors, professional organisations and other groups who participate in the governance of the domain) in 'crossing points' – those spaces where policymakers and scientists meet, talk and deliberate – that provoke phenomena of ideational alignment, ways of knowing and approaching policy problems that become common to everyone. Ideational alignment acts as a second mechanism of stabilisation, which embeds together the reflections of experts, policymakers and other governance actors. Third, experts can themselves *calibrate* the knowledge they produce, in order to adjust it to the needs of a given policy debate. Experts know that in order to be heard, they need to present solutions tied to broadly perceived possibilities of action. Under conditions of conflict, when actors try to push for their preferences, experts may also be pressed to find a compromise acceptable to all in order to make policy possible.

The theoretical argument of this book was developed through a dialogue between theory and empirical analysis of the production and mobilisation of ethics expertise in the EU context. EU policymakers have widely mobilised the expert bioethicists working for the European Group on Ethics in Science and New Technologies (EGE) – the European Union's (EU) own group of ethics experts, set up in 1991 to provide assistance on the ethical implications of biotechnology. Since its creation, the group has issued opinions on the ethical principles that should guide decisions in fields such as human genetics, cloned meat and agriculture, biometrics and new technologies such as nanomedicine. It has largely asserted itself as the authoritative expert body when ethical issues are openly debated.

The creation of the EGE was presented as a response to the need to enlarge participation to decision-making beyond traditional scientific groups. The group is, indeed, composed not only of scientists in the traditional sense, but also of theologians, philosophers and lawyers, all trained in ethics or bioethics, who are deemed better able to issue informed opinions on the ethical aspects of EU policies.[38] But despite the multi-disciplinarity of its members, and the rhetoric used by the European Commission in this respect, the creation of the group does not institute participation beyond specialists into decision-making. The EGE's sessions are private and participation of civil society representatives is allowed only during occasional roundtables, the outcome of which does not have to be reflected in the EGE's final opinion.

Due to the weakness of the EU's political resources linked to culture and universal suffrage and the lack of consensus amongst political and social actors on how to deal with sensitive decisions related to scientific and technological advances, the EU represents an ideal terrain to examine the mobilisation and production of ethical expertise. This book examines three policy domains: nanotechnology policy, data protection and embryo research. Each case varies in conflict intensity. In the case of nanotechnology the conflict is potential; in the field of data protection the conflict surfaced only after ethics experts had started working on their opinions; in the case of embryonic research the conflict was patent and hard to disentangle.

Implications

The Enmeshment of Expertise and Politics

The first implication is clear: at least when knowledge is mandated for the needs of policy, it lacks independence. Social scientists have used a range of concepts – such as regulatory science, mandated science or even applied science – to describe a form of knowledge that is constructed and negotiated for the needs of policy.[39] Policymakers mandate experts in a wide array of policy domains. In scientific and technological policymaking, expert groups are asked to evaluate risks related to new

---

[38] With six members at its inception, the EGE expanded to nine in 1994. From 1998 on, the EGE consisted of twelve members, including experts in sociology and informatics, who initially served terms of three years before increasing to four from 2000 on. Membership expanded to fifteen in 2005 and encompassed additional expertise in food safety and pharmacology. See the Annex in the book for a full list of EGE experts and their field of specialisation from 1991 to 2019.

[39] Jasanoff 1990; Irwin et al. 1997.

medicines, chemical contamination through food, or pollution control technologies. Beyond these domains, experts are mandated to evaluate risks associated with new financial products, recidivist criminal behaviour, or terrorism. Such groups are the 'channel through which regulatory acts and non-acts are negotiated, through which products diffuse, or fail to, the one through which policy objectives of protecting health and the environment or of sustaining innovation, are pursued'.[40] Existing research on 'regulatory science' has evidenced its inability to grasp signals of upcoming failures or disasters, problems of conflicts of interests, technological bias or phenomena of regulatory capture. The book sheds light on the way experts are enmeshed with politics (and sometimes with the industry) through tangible and clearly identifiable mechanisms. The mechanisms of stabilisation revealed in the book show how common ways of seeing problems amongst the actors involved in the governance of a given domain arise, but also prevent the possibility of dissenting voices being heard.[41]

Groups of ethics experts have, for their part, been portrayed as more deliberative and pluralistic forums, and as such as a means to check some of these ills – such as the propensity of policymakers and traditional scientific experts to non-reflectively promote innovation, either for scientistic or economic motives. The revealing of their enmeshment with those who do policy alerts us to their inability to play such roles. This is problematic from a democratic perspective, especially if they are mobilised to deal with issues perceived as contentious by the public. We observe, thus, the persistence of expert systems, even hidden under the cloak of deliberative procedures.[42]

---

[40] Demortain 2017, p. 142.
[41] Existing research has contrasted the knowledge such experts produce to conventional 'academic science', seen as more objective, autonomous and 'pure' from political and social inferences. It would, however, be an oversimplification to present such knowledge against an idealised form of research produced within the walls of universities. While interactions between experts and policy or experts and industry are more evident and occur through distinct mechanisms when expertise is mandated for policy, politicisation can occur via more indirect and diffuse processes in the case of academic research. Policymakers usually have less means to 'orchestrate' academic research, but the setting of research priorities by funding agencies makes for a significant caveat to this claim. Even when knowledge is not mandated for the needs of policy, researchers are inevitably influenced by ideas, debates and generally accepted criteria of what is considered to be worthwhile and valid knowledge at given times and places.
[42] See also Abels and Bora 2004.

Emerging Notions of Expertise

This book shows that what constitutes expert knowledge is far from static, and is the outcome of specific socio-political circumstances and the professional and political agendas which actors unfold in specific domains. We ought to pay attention, thus, to the epistemic and political contests over what knowledge is considered as 'expert', scientific or valid.

The emergence of ethics expertise bestows a specific authority in morals upon specialists. In dealing with the role of 'experts' or 'specialists' in the field of bioethics, the book brings to light the way a new type of expert knowledge has emerged and institutionalised itself in universities and as a key provider of advice for policy. The development of bioethics in the 1970s–1980s in the United States was enmeshed with politics; while bioethics became part of the curriculum of some schools of medicine, and autonomous bioethics institutes were also set in place, thus shaping its contours as that of an autonomous discipline, it also responded to a specific political demand for that kind of expertise. Policymakers who started to heavily recruit bioethicists for the needs of policy also shaped the contours of what bioethics could be.

Fundamentally, the fabric of ethics expertise is a story of expansion of the frontiers of expert authority over a contested ontological domain – the ethical analysis of medical, scientific and technological developments. The making of a new class of experts, who claimed to have the capacity to deliberate on the values at stake in biomedical research and scientific advances, has removed this task from the remit of scientists, who before had been perceived as solely responsible for deciding on the ethical value of their activities. It has also pushed back the claims of other professions, such as priests or theologians, to such analysis. By presenting ethics expertise as a more neutral, universal way of approaching ethical questions, ethics experts were able to sideline religious figures as 'non-scientific' and community-based, rather than universal, ethical analysis. The fabric of ethics expertise finally delegitimised claims that citizens themselves, lay patients and consumers were to have their say on such issues. By defining themselves as 'experts' – holders of specialist, neutral, universal knowledge – bioethicists contributed to the exclusion of various non-expert voices from debates on scientific and technological innovations. The creation of these new 'neutral specialists' delegitimised rival authorities such as doctors or scientists themselves (too enmeshed with their own activities), theologians (who can only talk in the name of religion) or citizens (who lack the expertise), thus expanding the boundaries of expert authority or what is presented as such on ethical reasoning. As such it testifies to the dynamic – and political – character of what is perceived as 'expert' and what is disqualified as 'non-expert', 'non-scientific', 'biased', 'religious' or 'militant science'.

Structure of the Book

Chapter 2 reviews, first, the literature on the nature of the relationship between knowledge and politics, bringing some of its shortcomings into light. It then develops a framework which captures how expertise is produced and mobilised in policy, making the case that the relationship between knowledge and politics, or expertise and policy, is stabilised through three forms of iteration, which I label 'orchestration', 'ideational alignment' and 'calibration'. As the production of expertise takes place in an iterative space in between knowledge and policy, such expertise can then itself become a stabilisation mechanism. Finally, the chapter focuses on the specificities of bioethical expertise, shedding light on its double-edged authority and the way its mobilisation plays out in the pre-emption or taming of conflicts on scientific and technological developments.

Chapter 3 retraces the development of ethics expertise both in domestic contexts and in global governance arenas. It goes back to the first debates on the need to include a social and ethical assessment of science and technology in the late 1970s in the United States, in the context of new social challenges presented by technological innovations (such as organ transplantation), the publicising of several instances of bad practice on the part of medical professionals, and risks that arose when molecular biologists discovered they could create DNA sequences in the laboratory that did not exist in nature. In this context, isolated scientists and politicians, theologians and groups of engaged citizens felt the need for the regulation of medical and scientific activities. But while concerns over the ethics of medicine and science were initially voiced as a strong critique, bioethics eventually took the form of a new expert discourse, which became entangled with politics. This genealogy of the emergence of the notion of bioethical expertise is key to understanding the function payed by such experts in policymaking today.

Chapter 4 examines the case of the EU controversy on embryo research. Although the EU's competences in the field of embryo research are limited to questions such as patent law and research funding, in practice debates on these specific aspects of biotechnology policy have induced more fundamental discussions on the status of the human embryo, with member states, interest groups and civil society actors defending fundamentally irreconcilable positions. Focusing on the two EGE opinions issued during the negotiations on the funding of human embryonic stem cell research (EGE 2000, 2007a), the chapter argues that the mobilisation of ethics experts allowed policymakers to successfully bypass the conflict on embryo research that had exploded in the context of EU research funding policy. The mobilisation of the EGE facilitated the technicalisation of discussions on embryo research, by shifting the debate away from the 'either/or' positions that had been voiced until then and presenting a range of intermediary scenarios. The EGE acted as a locus for the elaboration of a workable policy solution, when no closure of the controversy had been possible in the political arena. The position of ethics experts could then be invoked by EU policymakers in order to guide policy discussions and eventually justify the funding of hESC research in the absence of agreement amongst EU states. The European Commission was able to mobilise expert bioethicists to such avail because the position of the experts was very close to that of the European Commission. Policymakers and expert bioethicists worked together in various crossing points and developed a similar approach to the issue. Expert bioethicists also calibrated the knowledge they produced, in order to meet the expectations of the policy process. When the debate reopened ahead of the adoption of the EU Seventh Framing Programme (FP7), EU policymakers then carefully orchestrated the process of knowledge production by delineating strictly the questions experts were asked.

Chapter 5 examines the case of EU nanotechnology policy. In 2005, the European Commission asked the EGE to examine the ethical implications of nanomedicine. Here the mobilisation of ethics experts acted as a crucial tool to check the rise of a potential political conflict, and successfully did so. For EU policymakers, it was crucial that the 'push for nanos' did not meet citizens' concerns and protests. By showcasing that a new type of experts representing a diversity of voices had been consulted, the European Commission in fact ensured that policy remained formulated within a closed community composed of EU officials, experts and the industry. By asking the EGE to focus solely on ethical issues in the field of nanomedicine, the Commission also successfully framed other environmental and health safety concerns as technical, rather than ethical, issues – best dealt with through an improvement of existing tests than legislative reforms – thus allowing for a compartmentalisation of ethics and a technicalisation of the debate. The mobilisation of ethics experts acted as a stabilisation mechanism because expert knowledge was produced in an iterative process between experts and policymakers. EU policymakers gave substantial information to the EGE experts, informing them about the tenets of the policy debate as well as their own policy preferences. But orchestration was also facilitated by the embedding of experts into ongoing policy debates and narratives. EU policymakers and ethics experts worked together in various crossing points, such as the Bureau of European Policy Advisors (BEPA), conferences, workshops or roundtables – where a common way of looking at policy issues was developed.

Chapter 6 examines the case of the EU controversy on data protection. In May 2011 in the context of two sensitive policy reforms, the launch of the Digital Agenda for Europe, aimed at stimulating digital technology innovation and economic competitiveness, and the introduction of sensitive security and defence areas (related to biosecurity and cybersecurity in particular) in EU-funded research, the European Commission asked ethics experts to issue two opinions on the ethics of information and communication technologies (ICTs), signalling an 'ethics creep' to issues that fell outside the typical bioethical territory of ethics committees. Concerned that both policy items might provoke protests from the civil society, the European Commission mobilised ethics experts in order to check the rise of a potential policy conflict. But as the EGE experts started working on their opinions, the Commission also launched the data protection legislative reform; in this context data privacy became the object of a heated controversy, affecting both the thinking of the experts and the role they fulfilled in the policy process in various ways. First, the EGE became a terrain of competition between the various Commission Directorate Generals (DGs) involved in data protection issues. Each DG tried to present its own narrative of the policy problem to the EGE and *orchestrate* its work. As some DGs became more actively involved with the work of ethics experts, their concerns were also better reflected in the output of the EGE, especially when it resonated well with the concerns of the experts. With the sudden emergence of a sense of crisis around the Snowden revelations on US surveillance activities, the policy debate shifted towards the issue of surveillance. As positions became increasingly polarised, the EGE was also perceived as a terrain where the controversy could be closed. The EGE experts *calibrated* their findings in order to reconcile the conflicting objectives of the various DGs and provide policymakers with a more consensual narrative. The EGE's second opinion deconstructs binary positions that had been evoked in the debate and elaborates a more consensual policy narrative. The case brings to light that when policy conflicts intensify, the role of ethics experts shifts from conflict containment to conflict manoeuvring.

Chapter 7 offers concluding reflections. After briefly comparing the findings of the above cases, it considers their broader reach through a preliminary exploration of the mobilisation of ethics experts in the case of synthetic biology of the United States. It then connects the argument of the book to the literature on the politics of ethics in international relations (IR), making it clear that the expertisation of ethics has in fact allowed for a more efficient political mobilisation of ethics. It finally points to the crucial relevance of the book's findings to existing debates on the making of knowledge, agendas and policies in global governance.

2 Re-conceptualising the Enmeshment of Knowledge and Politics

This book asks how the notion of ethical expertise has emerged, what role its mobilisation plays in the governance of scientific and technological innovation and how this kind of expertise is produced. Addressing three questions in one manuscript is not an easy endeavour, especially when coming to the point of thinking of an analytical framing. The writing process has been one of trial and error, navigating between different literatures and continuous adjustment. Eventually I decided that these questions could be best addressed by thinking about the relationship between science, or knowledge, and politics as an enmeshed one. The two spheres are neither clearly distinct and autonomous, as widely assumed in the international relations (IR) or political science literature, nor indistinguishable, as assumed by STS scholars who see the relationship between knowledge and politics as one which is co-produced or co-constituted.

Existing literature in IR, comparative politics or public policy typically see knowledge and politics as two strictly separated spheres and has essentially focused on the question of whether, and under what conditions, experts influence policy. In doing so, it fails to capture mechanisms of interaction between the two spheres. The concept of co-production developed in STS provides us, for its part, with a useful lens to see the way knowledge 'embeds and is embedded in social practices, identities, norms, conventions, discourses, instruments and institutions'.[1] The analytical framing of the book is informed by this concept in that it focuses on the tangled relationship between knowledge and politics, but it also engages critically with its lack of attention to phenomena of agency, conflict and change, all central to the policy process. Co-production scholars have focused on macro-level dynamics through which state narratives and certain forms of knowledge are co-constituted. It needs translation to capture what stabilises

---

[1] Jasanoff 2004, pp. 2–3.

(or destabilises) the relationship between knowledge and politics at the meso-level analysis of policy processes.

With its focus on the process of co-legitimation between knowledge and the social, or expertise and politics, co-production does not really capture moments when things seem to be falling apart. In such moments of destabilisation, existing narratives and the governance modes which embody them become explicitly contested. The types of expertise that existing governance modes rely on can also become publicly debated and criticised, and subject to renegotiation, thus leaving the door open for new forms of knowledge to emerge and be heard, and for others to become disregarded.

Conversely, co-production does not help us understand how governance narratives, their associated governance modes and the kinds of expertise they rely on are stabilised despite the presence of (explicit, implicit or potential) conflict that is endemic to the policy process. Jasanoff acknowledges that hegemonic forces are the '(co)-products of contingent interactions and practices',[2] and thus, that stability or co-legitimation between science and politics is not a given. But co-production does not trace such interactions at the level of policy processes, in which, even during seemingly stable periods of time after or before moments of destabilisation, conflict might be underlying, intentionally avoided, contained or dissimulated. The co-legitimation of science and politics in fact occurs via the operating of specific forms of iteration between the two spheres, which produce ideational alignment between experts, policymakers and other governance actors so that recognised forms of knowledge and expertise do not depart policymakers' agendas.

I argue here that the relationship between knowledge and politics, or expertise and policy, is stabilised through three forms of iteration, which I label 'orchestration', 'ideational alignment' and 'calibration'. Orchestration refers to the way policymakers (or other governance actors) try to *orchestrate* the production of expert knowledge in order to make it more favourable to their agendas, thus directly trying to stabilise the content and form of recognised knowledge. But strategic orchestration is facilitated by autonomous mechanisms. Policymakers may find experts to be very receptive interlocutors because they work together with them in various crossing points – arenas where

---

[2] Jasanoff 2004, p. 36.

policymakers and experts meet, work and reflect together until a phenomenon of *ideational alignment* occurs. Ideational alignment refers to this coming together of all actors around certain ways of seeing problems. Finally, calibration refers to the way experts themselves may calibrate the knowledge they produce in order to meet the needs of the policy process. Looking at the emergence and production of expertise through the lens of these three concepts allows us to specify the mechanisms of co-production at the meso-level of the policy process and reveal the specific mechanisms via which ideational alignment between science and politics occurs during the making of policy.

After introducing the main insights in existing literatures, as well as their limitations, this chapter makes explicit how the framework developed here aims to contribute to these. In a typical instance of theory building taking place in between inductive case study work and theoretical reflections, it develops an analytical framework to elucidate the dynamics of emergence and production of expertise in global governance. In a final section it focuses on the specificities of bioethical expertise, shedding light on its double-edged authority and the way its mobilisation plays a unique role in the pre-emption or taming of conflicts on scientific and technological developments.

Knowledge and Politics: Overview of the Literature

Existing approaches argue either that policymakers resort to expertise in order to inform and guide policy or that policymakers are strategic actors who control processes of knowledge production, by producing expert knowledge themselves or shaping the way it is produced in other arenas. These assumptions have resulted in the development of research programmes that assume that science and policy belong to strictly separated spheres.

The Rationality Project

Existing research on the role of expertise in policymaking has long assumed, and often still does, that policymakers resort to expert knowledge in order to improve the quality of policy choices. As much in the field of IR as in comparative politics or public policy, most accounts of science–policy relations remain informed by a rationalist assumption, according to which decision makers mobilise expertise in order to rationalise governance.³ What has been labelled the 'rationality project' emerged amongst political scientists back in the 1950s, when a group of scholars developed hopes that policymakers would advance better policy agendas and programmes if they used sound evidence in the formulation of their decisions.⁴ Lasswell and Kaplan famously put forward this argument in an essay that argues that if science produces true and valid knowledge, this will also produce the right political decisions when such knowledge is used.⁵ From this perspective the development of scientific knowledge is driven by the logic of science, independently of the circumstances of time, place and social conditions. And if it is possible to discover and apprehend reality by 'getting down to the facts', the application of science-based knowledge would, indeed, seem to be the best way to help with solving policy problems. Social scientists who adhered to this vision took it as a task to make their discipline a tool that would improve the rationality of decision-making, and were swift to dismiss politics, which appeared to them as an obstacle to rational and well-founded policy.⁶

Because most political scientists share such rationalist assumptions, they are exclusively concerned with the influence – or lack of it – of expert knowledge on policy. In what can be seen as an early version of an argument later developed by Haas, Weiss in her 'enlightenment model' highlights that knowledge shapes or alters decision makers' understanding of given issues. 'Research provides a background of data, empirical generalisations, and ideas that affect the way policymakers think about problems'.⁷ From this standpoint, research-based ideas gradually influence the way in which problems and issues are understood and eventually addressed.⁸

This focus on the effects of expert knowledge very much prevails in the analysis of global governance. IR scholars have argued that because they deal with highly complex and technical issues, international decision makers are highly dependent on science and technology for determining the risks and consequences associated with political action. In *When Knowledge Is Power*, Haas sheds light on how 'invisible colleges' of like-minded professionals from different disciplines could, at times, influence

---

[3] Haas 1992; Meyer et al. 1997.   [4] See, for instance, Stone 2012; Weiss 1977.
[5] Lasswell and Kaplan 1950.
[6] See, for instance, Lane 1962; Bell 1960. See also Daviter 2015 for an account of the rationality project.
[7] Weiss 1982, p. 621.   [8] Weiss 1979; Weiss and Bucuvalas 1980.

international organisations, which, however, remain fundamentally habit driven.[9] In 1992, the 'epistemic communities' concept entered the mainstream of IR scholarship with Peter Haas's analysis of the role of experts in promoting international policy coordination. Policy ambiguity creates uncertainty in decision makers' minds, and as a result they seek information to inform their choices.[10] This search enables an epistemic community to provide information that excludes or enhances different alternatives. This approach has stimulated a research programme which seeks to identify the scope conditions of the influence of research on policy and identifying obstacles that prevent a better flow of scientific research to policymaking.[11] But the mobilisation of experts by policymakers does not always result from the expectation that more or better evidence helps to solve given policy problems.

Political Uses of Expertise

Alternative accounts focus on the mobilisation of knowledge for political purposes. It does not take a great knowledge of politics, indeed, to notice that policymakers often invoke scientific research either in order to support their policy proposals or to legitimise their political authority. Existing research has evidenced that policymakers use expert knowledge in order to back their political preferences.[12] Weiss points out that knowledge can be mobilised 'to support a predetermined position'.[13] When expertise is used in order to support particular policy programmes we can observe a politicisation of expertise which then becomes 'ammunition for the side that finds its conclusions congenial or supportive'.[14] The political use of expertise is often associated with political behaviour that uses analytical information 'selectively and often distortingly',[15] in which the use of knowledge is distorted, manipulated and shaped by the dynamics of the political process. When there is a political conflict, opposed actors or coalitions are particularly likely to mobilise expert knowledge as a weapon to gain control over the framing of issues at stake, and eventually policy outcomes.[16] From this perspective, expertise plays a role but more as

---

[9] Haas 1990, p. 45.   [10] Haas 1992.
[11] See, for instance, Verdun 1999; Zito 2001; Elvins 2003; Haas and Stevens 2011.
[12] Weiss 1977; Benveniste 1972; Nelkin 1975.   [13] Weiss 1977, p. 15.
[14] Weiss 1979, p. 429.   [15] Knorr 1977, p. 171.
[16] Boswell 2009; or see Schrefler 2010.

it feeds into claims concerning the contours and classification of policy problems. A number of scholars have pointed out that governance is about problems which are ill-defined, ambiguous and indeterminate. Policymakers deal with messy 'paradoxes' which cannot be approached through the exercise of instrumental rationality. For Stone, 'it is impossible to extricate policy from the "messy" world of politics' because 'reasoned analysis ... always involves choices to include some things and exclude others and to view the world in a particular way when other visions are possible'.[17] In such circumstances, stakeholders do not only resort to existing expertise, but can also engage in the production of counter-expertise, as a means to undermine the position of their opponents. What matters then is not the quality of the evidence provided; it is often sufficient to discredit the evidence presented by the political adversaries.[18] Existing literature has revealed the way policymakers use expert knowledge selectively – and sometimes misleadingly – in order to back their agendas and programmes, frame issues in a way that pushes the policy solutions they prefer, gain legitimacy or expand their competences.[19]

These insights are useful and capture important facets of the strategic mobilisation of expertise in the policymaking process, but they miss some important dynamics of the production and mobilisation of expert knowledge. Much of the literature, indeed, assumes that expertise is first produced and then enters into politics (the 'enlightenment' or 'rationalist' model described above), or that policymakers fully control processes of knowledge use, and orient it with the aim of pursuing specific interests (the 'political uses of knowledge' model described in this section). Such accounts conceive of knowledge and policy as belonging to two separated spheres. In doing so, they fail to capture iterations between the two spheres.

The Co-production of Knowledge

Scholars in science and technology studies (STS) have for their part long pointed out that scientific activity is 'located within academic, industrial and governmental settings'.[20] Latour, for instance, has argued that scientific knowledge enjoys no independence or claim to authority

---

[17] Stone 2012, p. 375.   [18] Nelkin 1975.
[19] Weiss 1979, p. 429; Littoz-Monnet 2017.   [20] Irwin et al. 1997, p. 22.

beyond the political and economic interests which helped develop the scientific claims.[21] From that perspective science 'embeds and is embedded in social practices, identities, norms, conventions, discourses, instruments and institutions'.[22] Science and politics coproduce one another; not only are political interactions based on available knowledge, but the production of scientific knowledge is itself determined by its political and social context. Citing Jasanoff, coproduction examines 'how knowledge-making is incorporated into practices of governance' and in reverse 'how practices of governance influence the making and use of knowledge'.[23] This perspective makes it difficult to demarcate science and politics at all and thus investigate the link between knowledge and politics or policymaking. Posing the theoretical question of how knowledge and decision-making are linked becomes an anomalous query that cannot be answered. That knowledge is at once a product and a producer of forms of social life is difficult to deny. But while knowledge is indeed always produced in a given political, ideological and social context, the co-production lens tends to leave aside phenomena of agency, contestation and conflict, and potential co-optation. Its focus on macro-level dynamics through which state identities or narratives and certain knowledge forms are coproduced needs translation to capture the contingent interactions between knowledge and politics at the meso-level analysis of policy processes, in which actors and conflict (whether fostered by material or ideational factors) are central.

In particular, the lens of co-production does not help us understand moments of *destabilisation*, when things seem to be falling apart, and kinds of expertise formerly considered valid and relevant are being questioned. How are political narratives and the associated governance frameworks and the expertise they rely on ever contested if knowledge and the social are always co-produced?

In the same way, co-production needs translation to capture the specific meso-level mechanisms that produce stability. I argue that the relationship between science and politics in fact needs to be *stabilised*, so that potential contestation does not occur and conflict is avoided. Ideational alignment, and thus co-legitimation between knowledge and

---

[21] Latour 1987. See also Litfin 1994; Callon et al. 2009. On the relationship between science and the state, see the seminal works from Foucault 1978 and Scott 1998.
[22] Jasanoff 2004, pp. 2–3.   [23] Jasanoff 2004, p. 3.

politics, is the product of specific forms of iterations between these two spheres, which are not only analytically distinguishable but also (often) empirically observable. Such questions are key, because without addressing them it is difficult to understand both *change* – of governance modes and the kinds of expertise they rely on – and *dynamics of stability*, in spite of underlying (or more explicit) conflicts between actors even in seemingly stable circumstances.

Expertise and Politics: between Stabilisation and Destabilisation

Narratives, Governance Modes and Knowledge

A governance narrative is an ideational framework that guides policy-makers and informs their agendas. It encompasses certain assumptions about the functioning of social reality, what goals are worth pursuing and what problems are worth being addressed. A governance narrative is a kind of storytelling in specific times and places, which make sense of a complex reality and guides political action. Narratives empower certain groups, silence others, and also determine what kinds of conflicts are likely to emerge. Existing accounts on the role of ideas have also discussed how broader values, whether they are termed as 'worldviews',[24] 'public moods'[25] or 'wider societal concerns',[26] define social reality. While there is a resonance between governance narratives and broader societal values, our interest here focuses on the more specific narratives which guide political action in specific policy domains.

When a narrative becomes dominant in a given policy domain, it becomes embodied in specific governance modes. Governance modes are defined here as governance arrangements that empower certain actors and disenfranchise others and rely on specific governance techniques and forms of expertise, which become accepted by all or are at least not explicitly questioned. Governance modes might be more bureaucratic or instead more democratic, based on binding regulatory mechanisms or instead on self-regulation, and involve different types of actors in the formulation of policy decisions. Each governance mode can rely on specific governance techniques – such as reliance on indicators, evaluations, predictive models, the use of policy diffusion mechanisms and project policy (when every problem is tackled through

[24] Goldstein 1993. [25] Jacobsen 1995. [26] Rhinard 2010.

the creation and completion of time-limited 'projects') – and on specific forms of knowledge. Governance actors can rely on a diversity of knowledge forms. In global governance, reliance on expert knowledge is ubiquitous. International organisations and domestic bureaucracies alike rely on highly technical forms of knowledge produced by economists and statisticians.[27] Risk evaluation in various domains of science and technology governance is for its part provided by scientists from an array of different disciplines. Private actors are also increasingly called in as 'experts' in policy formulation, be it in the domains of finance, health or security.[28] Testifying to this turn, private consultancy firms often act as knowledge providers for domestic governments or international bureaucracies. But other forms of knowledge are also increasingly accepted as relevant for policy. 'Civil society' concerns have been better integrated into policy decisions and diverse experiments such as consensus conferences, citizen panels and related mechanisms are being explored, all acknowledging the value of lay knowledge in policy processes.[29] Given the evident interconnection between narratives, modes of governance and the types of expertise that policymakers rely on, the creation of certain types of expertise or simply the coming to prominence of formerly ignored forms of knowledge cannot be examined independently of broader ideational and governance contexts.

Moments of Destabilisation and the Reordering of Expertise

Expertise is not 'created' or 'produced' in response to specific and objective problems. The rise of new forms of expertise – such as bioethical expertise – or the fading of existing ones occurs when existing governance narratives and the more concrete governance arrangements that embody them are destabilised or thrown into question. An emerging body of literature is concerned with the emergence of new fields of expertise. Often inspired by Abbott, who in his seminal work *The System of Professions*[30] has focused on conflicts amongst different occupational groups, existing accounts focus on the micro-dynamics that characterise struggles internal to specific professions or networks

---

[27] Reinalda and Verbeek 2003; Barnett and Finnemore 2004.
[28] Tsingou 2015; Demortain 2015; Berndtsson 2012.   [29] Guston 1999.
[30] Abbott 1988.

of experts or amongst several of these groups. Conceiving expertise as a network, 'linking together agents, devices, concepts, and institutional and spatial arrangements'[31] which can be 'rewired', Eyal examines how the parents of autistic children were able to forge 'an alternative network of expertise' challenging the monopoly of clinicians, where new autism expertise was formed through 'a team or an actor-network composed of therapists, psychologists, psychiatrists, and parents, with the latter occupying the leading role'.[32] Gendron et al. in their study of the emergence and consolidation of auditing expertise argue that the construction of a new form of expert knowledge is 'a project of fact building that involves the construction of networks of support'.[33] It is through the emergence, consolidation and sustaining of networks of expertise that knowledge becomes understood as universal and even natural. Such accounts trace how specific domains or forms of expertise are gradually assembled.

But the rewiring of networks in the scientific, expert and even professional spheres needs to be connected to broader historical, societal or ideational changes. New kinds of expertise emerge or gain credibility when governance narratives and the governance modes that embody them become destabilised and the kinds of knowledge traditionally considered valid become contested. We need, thus, to connect the micro to the macro and examine the emergence or the dismissal of specific forms of expertise, in connection to shifts at the broader level of governance narratives and the arrangements that embody them. Put differently, new forms of knowledge emerge when the relationship between politics and knowledge becomes unstable, leaving room for alternative forms of knowledge to gain ground.

Doing so requires paying more attention to moments of destabilisation, when existing frameworks that were once taken for granted become an object of debate and contestation. Best refers to moments when settled assumptions become the subject of problematisation, when certain issues come to be viewed 'as matters of concern, either for the first time or in new ways'.[34] Events, technical or scientific discoveries and innovations, the publicisation of new 'facts' in the media, the activism of specific groups which bring new problems to light, and the role of entrepreneurial policymakers can all contribute to

---

[31] Eyal 2013, p. 863. [32] Eyal 2013, p. 886. [33] Gendron et al. 2007, p. 101.
[34] Best 2014, p. 26.

the destabilisation of existing political frameworks or compromises. Jasanoff in her work refers to the role of disruptive moments – such as the birth of the cloned sheep Dolly in Scotland – but denies the ability of such events to 'dictate the pathways along which public responses will move'.[35] Birkland prefers the term 'focusing events' to refer to sudden, uncommon events, such as disasters, failures or major changes which take place in a given issue domain.[36] Whether called 'disruptive', or 'focusing', such events, although they indeed do not play a deterministic role, provoking changes which simply logically respond to them, can *destabilise normal ways of thinking and doing things*. Ideational changes are often provoked by specific material events, innovations and failures which unsettle existing ideas.[37] Governance narratives, their associated modes of governance and forms of recognised expertise do not evolve in a vacuum and can be challenged by specific material developments.

As in other domains in which expert or scientific authority has been challenged and new forms of expertise have gained ground – such as Eyal's study of autism, where the expert authority of scientists was replaced by that of educational therapists and lay experts, or Best's study of global development finance, where a new kind of 'provisional' expertise has gained ground – bioethical expertise has emerged at a time when formerly acknowledged forms of expertise have come under challenge. The assumption of scientific autonomy, that scientists themselves are the most capable and legitimate experts to decide on the right or wrong of their activities, was thrown into question by the mediatisation of questionable scientific practices and technological advances. Citizens, reflexive scientists and some activists voiced the opinion that scientific developments do not always work for the good, thus challenging the dominant pro-science and innovation narrative, and the associated idea that scientists were best equipped to decide on their own activities. It was amidst this general sense that existing ways of doing things needed renegotiation that bioethics emerged.

But the creation of bioethical *expertise* also led to the co-optation of citizens' protests by specialists. Bioethics became an expert discourse, and its mainstream version was stabilised around a specific set of doctrines which allowed for the pro-science and innovation narrative to essentially persist, *with* the support of bioethics. New

[35] Jasanoff 2005, p. 24. [36] Birkland 1998. [37] Best 2017.

governance frameworks may rely on new governance techniques or new forms of expertise, but if dominant narratives are not fundamentally challenged the changes may actually act as *mechanisms of stabilisation* of former frameworks, even when presented under another guise.

Stabilisation Mechanisms: Orchestration, Ideational Alignment and Calibration

Existing governance arrangements – relying on specific kinds of expertise – can be contested, making the relationships between science and politics unstable. Even during seemingly stable periods of time, the co-legitimation of science and politics is not self-evident. Conflict might be underlying, contained or dissimulated. Specific forms of iterations between knowledge and politics produce ideational alignment between experts, policymakers and other governance actors so that recognised forms of knowledge and expertise do not depart from policy-makers' agendas. I argue here that the logics of orchestration, ideational alignment and calibration act as stabilisation mechanisms and ensure that the relationship between knowledge and politics remains stable so that co-legitimation between the two spheres can operate.

Orchestration: The logic of orchestration allows us to capture the way policymakers may develop tactics to shape the production of knowledge and ensure that experts do not develop counter-narratives. Experts have their own agency and may develop their own ideas or discourses that do not systematically echo dominant narratives. Policymakers may thus develop strategies to ensure that experts do not diverge from their own agendas. Of course, they can do this by picking up and choosing certain experts and leaving others aside. Alternative voices are thus excluded from decision-making processes and kept silent. Policymakers can also produce 'in-house' expertise when they work for a bureaucratic organisation with such capacities and pick and choose which experts are consulted or hired. They may also try to directly influence the experts hired or consulted, for instance, by feeding experts with their own data and evidence about the issues at stake or asking them specific questions. Mitchell et al. argue that expert knowledge has influence to the extent that policymakers 'educate scientists about their concerns, values, priorities, resources, and knowledge of the problem'.[38] Policymakers can also influence experts by outlining what the contours of the policy debate are – or at least with their own definition of what these contours are – thus clearly delineating what the possible alternatives seem to be. They can thus present their own position, the position of the relevant actors in the domain at stake, and their own portrayal of bargaining constraints and acceptable policy scenarios. Orchestration is ubiquitous in the case of experts working in think tanks or for expert groups mandated by policymakers. It acts as a stabilisation strategy and ensures that dominant narratives are not contested

Crossing points and ideational alignment: Science is situated within broader political structures, but the relationship between science and politics needs to be stabilised. Our argument here points to the *non-automaticity* of embeddedness – as testified by the possibility of alternative discourses and counter-narratives. The development of common narratives and ways of thinking in given issue domains is *reinforced or stabilised through a logic of ideational alignment*. Ideational alignment exists when policymakers, experts and other participants in the policy process all share a common set of assumptions or a common governance narrative, but it emphasises that these are not just 'there' once and for all but develop and stabilise through specific forms of interactions. Common narratives are created or reinforced through repeated interactions in crossing points – those spaces where governance actors and experts meet, talk and deliberate. These crossing points can be work meetings, conferences, consultative forums, reflection forums or roundtables.[39] In these arenas, experts and policymakers develop common ways of knowing and approaching policy problems, which one may call 'policy theories', 'frames'[40] or 'policy knowledge'.[41] Kwak, for instance, has pointed out in relation to the evaluation of new technologies that given the social interactions amongst industries, experts and regulators, all develop a similar way of seeing problems.[42] Demortain has also shown that in the domain of toxicity

---

[38] Mitchell et al. 2006, p. 324; Penissat 2007.
[39] See, for instance, Robert 2010b on the way experts often share knowledge, competences and know-how with the policymakers they work with.
[40] On policy frames, see, for instance, Bachrach and Baratz 1962; Schön and Rein 1994; and more recently, Jones and Baumgartner 2004; Daviter 2009.
[41] Demortain 2017.   [42] Kwak 2014.

testing, a 'common fabric of assumptions and claims unites experts and policymakers, such as the notion that predictions of human safety can reliably be derived from tests on animals'.[43] The logic of ideational alignment better accounts for the way actors' positions are *brought into line* through repeated meetings in crossing points. The point is not to deny that experts may have some degree of autonomy and agency when they formulate their views on specific policy problems. The presence of 'dissenting opinions' in the reports produced by mandated expert groups shows that experts can, at times, resist the prevailing narratives.[44] Such resistance, however, is rare, and the repeated iterations between experts and policymakers tend to dilute differences and potential conflicts. The common assumptions and ideas constructed or stabilised in these crossing points result in certain ways of approaching problems becoming uncontested – thus compromising the viability of certain alternatives.

Calibration: Experts can themselves *calibrate* the expertise they produce, in order to adjust it to the needs of a given policy debate. First, when experts produce knowledge at the request of policymakers, they can calibrate their claims in order to adjust these out of an understanding that policymakers need to carry out their reforms or policy agendas.[45] Robert points out that policymakers direct specific expectations towards expert groups, such as being able to reach intellectual compromises and craft workable policy scenarios, and thus act as facilitators of policy.[46] Lindblom and Cohen, for their part, argue that for expert knowledge to have some practical use, scientific findings must be tied to possibilities for action, as well as policymakers' understanding of their latitude for action.[47] Experts, thus, are expected to show their awareness of existing political constraints and issue findings or recommendations that do not only inform policy, but also *support the policy process*, in the sense that they facilitate the adoption of policies and programmes.

Second, experts may also adjust their output in order to meet the conflicting requests of the political actors with whom they interact. Executives can be divided, and bureaucratic organisations are not monolithic units either; different sections of the same organisation or government may have conflicting views and preferences. Private actors

---

[43] Demortain 2017, p. 147. [44] Penissat 2007, p. 10. [45] Penissat 2007.
[46] Robert 2010a, p. 23. [47] Lindblom and Cohen 1979.

may also be very active participants to the policy process and interact with experts too. Experts may thus be subject to various sources of pressure and feel urged to present an output that is simply 'acceptable' to all actors in place. In such circumstances experts feel pressed to delineate scenarios that will permit policy to proceed. The logic of calibration refers to the way experts use their agency, but do so for the purpose of self-restraint, rather than that of contestation, once they act as advisors for politics.

These techniques of stabilisation ensure that the relationship between knowledge and politics remains stable. They result in certain kinds of knowledge becoming dominant and acting as legitimating devices for specific narratives and political agendas. For the governance of science and technological innovation, these stabilisation mechanisms have ensured that bioethics remains subservient to politics. They have shaped what *mainstream bioethics* could be. Mainstream bioethics does not diverge from the powerful 'progress through medical and scientific innovation' narrative. It is dominated by utilitarian considerations, based on balancing risks and benefits, which are compatible with a pro-science and market-oriented framing of scientific and technological issues. Bioethical knowledge is embodied within this narrative, but it also helps in stabilising it. In that sense there is a co-legitimation process of knowledge and politics. Although groups of citizens, theologians and bioethicists who do not adhere to mainstream doctrines in the field have contested the agenda of bioethics, orchestration, ideational alignment and calibration ensure the stabilisation of a certain version of bioethics.

Bioethical Expertise as Tool of Stabilisation

While the stabilisation mechanisms described above provide conceptual lenses to look at the relationship between science and politics more broadly, a zoom in on ethical expertise is necessary to reveal its specificities. Ethical expertise is unique, in that it is invested with a blended form of authority, which is both epistemic, like traditional forms of expertise, but also 'democratic' in that ethics bodies *claim* to represent a diversity of voices and moral positions. Because it is endowed with this blended form of authority it can also play a unique role in the governance of scientific and technological innovation.

On the one hand, groups made up of expert bioethicists benefit from an aura of diversity, reflectivity and an altogether more 'democratic' nature. Policymakers in pluralist democracies present ethics committees as a novel and more deliberative form of advisory mechanism. Ethics groups, indeed, include a greater diversity of disciplinary voices than other expert groups. They typically comprise scientists in a traditional sense – medical doctors trained in ethics, molecular biologists or neurologists who have added to their trajectory some form of training in medical ethics – but also philosophers, lawyers and on some occasions theologians (although this is not the case at the EU level). It is this disciplinary diversity that policymakers invoke in order to make the claim that they have consulted broadly and openly on the ethical implications of specific scientific and technological developments. Ethics groups, however, do not include any civil society representatives. All participants sit in such groups as experts, and not as activists or representatives of any societal group.

On the other hand, and in addition to making a claim to their diverse and deliberative nature, ethics experts take great care to present themselves as 'independent', 'objective' and 'neutral' possessors of specialist, academic knowledge. Most bioethicists see bioethical expertise as 'the ability to reason formally and consistently' and 'apply argumentative tools to moral issues and cases'.[48] The emergence of ethics expertise bestows, in fact, a specific authority in morals upon specialists who claim to be applying systematic and universal tools of analysis, presenting their knowledge as general and applicable to all circumstances. Bioethical expertise does not deal with 'facts' or 'evidence' like traditional scientific expertise, but it relies on the same claims to objective knowledge and epistemic authority. In its mainstream version, bioethics is an expert discourse which presents moral argumentation as a rational endeavour. The creation of expert bioethicists has 'scienticised' ethics through the creation of doctrines, concepts and a specialised terminology, thus legitimising the idea that moral problems could be addressed in a seemingly objective and rational way by experts. Not all bioethicists adhere to this rationalist framework, and voices outside of the recognised 'expert' sphere, such as theologians, philosophers who adhere to other frameworks, non-governmental organisations (NGOs), activists or even consumers, contest this way

---

[48] Sanchini 2015, p. 55.

of approaching bioethical issues. But these alternative voices are not consulted by policymakers and thus kept silent in policy debates.

Because expert bioethicists are invested with a blended form of authority, their mobilisation can play a unique role in the management of scientific and technological controversies when policymakers do not want their pro-science and innovation agendas to be contested.

The mobilisation of bioethics – at least in its stabilised mainstream version – in policymaking is itself a particularly *efficient technique of stabilisation*. It can help policymakers contain underlying conflicts before they surface, or alternatively bypass or tame existing ones when the public or dissenting voices have already engaged in protests. Because the seemingly participatory or democratic nature of ethical expertise can be invoked, policymakers can more easily pre-empt the expansion of policy debates to the broader public. Mechanisms of governance, presented as more 'inclusive', 'deliberative' or 'consultative' – such as ethics committees – can, precisely because they give an *appearance* of broader consultation and dialogue, help to ensure that policy remains insulated and no conflicts arise. Policy formulation can be kept under the control of a closed policy community of actors, typically made up of policymakers, interest groups and experts. When such actors control policy, debates take place behind closed doors and the public is excluded.[49] Of course, citizens can also become aware of the political implications of such activities and force the opening up of policy discussions. But the technicality of debates makes for a strong entry point and limits the ability of the public to participate.[50]

While claiming to be making the policy process more participatory, policymakers can at the same time claim to be governing rationally when they involve expert bioethicists in the policy process. Typically, discussions amongst experts are framed in a technical fashion. Experts typically see their role as that of moderate, reasonable and ultimately rational appraisers of given policy problems, rather than political advocates.[51] Ethics experts do not derogate to this; they see themselves as 'scientists', rather than advocates of specific values or ideas. As discussed above, mainstream bioethics

---

[49] See on this point Richardson and Jordan 1979; Rhodes and Marsh 1992; Hoppe 2005.
[50] Jordan and Maloney 1997.
[51] See, for instance, Abélès and Bellier 1996; Trépos 1996.

is dominated by utilitarian considerations, based on balancing risks and benefits, which can well be formulated in rational terms. Ethical expertise thus acts as a seemingly 'objective' assessment technique, which provides policymakers with an ideal resource to technicalise ethical debates. As argued by Nelkin, 'debate over technical alternatives need not weight conflicting interests, but only the relative effectiveness of various approaches for resolving an immediate problem'.[52] Scholars have shown that even issues such as abortion or cloning, which would seem to have a more manifest ethical component, can be framed in more procedural terms when one focuses, for instance, on the best methods or timeline for terminating a pregnancy through abortion, rather than the principle of abortion itself.[53] When discussions are delegated to experts, policy conflicts can thus often be maintained at an 'intermediate level' and focus on 'the definition of acceptable procedural rules', such as 'non-binding instruments, implementation arrangement and administrative rules'.[54] When issues are discussed in such terms, political choices are concealed behind the technicity of the language adopted. By making ethics a matter of expert judgement, a degree of complexity and technicality can be reintroduced into policy debates.

Finally, because ethical expertise explicitly expands the frontiers of expert authority over 'moral' issues, it also provides policymakers with a particularly effective tool to tame or even close such controversies (and not only those framed in scientific terms). Ethics groups provide a propitious terrain for the crafting of workable policy solutions. Not only is the tone of discussions more technical, but, as noted earlier, ethics experts also know that in order to be heard, they need to calibrate their claims and adjust them to the contours and criteria of a given policy debate. The knowledge experts produce therefore goes through a process of adjustment and calibration even before it enters the policy process. The solution delineated in the expert arena can then be presented as a legitimate end point to the public and all stakeholders involved, and as such help to close existing controversies.[55]

[52] Nelkin 1975, p. 36.
[53] Engeli and Varone 2011, p. 242. See literature on morality policies: Knill 2013; Mooney and Lee 2000; Baumgartner et al. 2008.
[54] Engeli and Varone 2011, p. 248.
[55] See, for instance, Jasanoff 2005; Littoz-Monnet 2015.

The remainder of the book will show how bioethics emerged at a time when the scientific self-government mode was destabilised (Chapter 3) and how it was subsequently stabilised in a science-friendly rationalist discourse, subservient to politics. The stabilisation techniques are examined in three empirical in-depth cases in which bioethical expertise was mobilised (Chapters 4, 5 and 6).

3 | *The Fabric of Ethics Experts*
A Genealogy of (Bio)Ethical Expertise

The emergence of ethics experts bestows a specific authority in morals upon specialists. This new category of professionals offers a new type of expert advice, which aims at guiding policy along the 'right' ethical path, rather than advising specific policy choices on grounds of scientific rationality. Their authority, however, remains based on claims to special knowledge; bioethicists speak as epistemic authorities, not moral ones, and legitimise their voice by referring to their education and training in systematic forms of ethical analysis. In what context and under what circumstances has the idea of 'ethical' or 'bioethical' expertise emerged? How could the notion of *expertise in moral analysis* assert itself and become accepted amongst policymakers, scientists and the public? How were other claims to jurisdiction over these questions – from scientists themselves, theologians or the public – sidelined?

This chapter makes the case that the emergence of expert bioethicists, initially a US phenomenon before reaching Europe and more recently non-Western countries, took place as a response to an array of interacting dynamics. New technological advances in genetic engineering, highly mediatised cases of heart transplants, as well as the revealing of highly questionable experiments on human subjects by doctors triggered unprecedented concerns with the ethics of medicine and scientific practices in the 1970s, destabilising the long-established idea that scientists were to decide on the morality of their own practices. A handful of self-reflective scientists, theologians, engaged politicians and critical citizens voiced their concerns that scientists should not be left to themselves to decide what kind of research to conduct and what scientific developments to promote. At the same time, however, the bulk of scientists opposed any idea of oversight on their work, strongly fighting what they saw as an encroachment on their jurisdiction and realm of expertise. Policymakers, who also started to heavily recruit bioethicists for the needs of policy, also shaped the contours of what bioethics could be. While concerns over the ethics of medicine and science were initially voiced as a strong critique, essentially from theologians, doctors with a strong religious inclination and informed citizens, it was essentially developed, with the support of policymakers, within the institutional structure of medicine and as a friendly form of overseeing. The emergence of a new caste of experts in ethics – with all the questions this may raise in itself – pushed aside the remit of scientists' jurisdiction, but it also delegitimised claims that citizens themselves, or other actors such as priests or theologians, were to have their say on such issues. This genealogy of the emergence of the notion of bioethical expertise is key to understanding the function played by such experts in policymaking today.

The first section of this chapter presents the scientific and medical advances that formed the context in which 'bioethical' debates emerged in the United States. While scientific practices caused discord well before the 1970s, the mediatisation at that time provoked broader questionings of established governance modes and put policymakers in a position to respond. The second section examines this moment of destabilisation, by examining debates within Congress and Senate over the necessity to control scientists' activities, the form this oversight may take and the setting in place of the first advisory bioethics commissions in the United States. The section then expands the analysis to Western Europe and, while acknowledging the specificities of social, historical and political circumstances in various domestic contexts, shows that bioethics advisory groups consistently made scientific advances possible, rather than hampered them. The third section explores the way bioethics emerged as an autonomous discipline within universities. While the emergence of bioethics degrees, journals and professional associations legitimised the idea that a new discipline – and thus a new form of expertise – was in the making, its strong enmeshment with the institutional structure of medical schools as well as bioethicists' spanning roles between academia and policy, ensured that its thrust provided scientists and policymakers with a friendly discourse.

Inventing Bioethics in the United States: A Moment of Destabilisation

In the 1970s, the revelation that doctors were conducting research experiments on human beings without their consent, as well as scientific advances in the field of genetic engineering and organ transplantation, triggered new questions about scientific practices, and whether doctors were to remain the sole authority to decide upon them. But the 'bioethical' nature of these questions was not self-evident; past medical practices bore the potential of being as controversial and yet did not result in an outbreak of public debates. This is a conjunction of several contextual factors, including the mediatisation of these controversies at a time when various groups were asking for a greater democratisation of politics, the role of entrepreneurial politicians, and the intersection of specific professional agendas which made the framing of these issues as 'bioethical' – and thus prone to external arbitration – possible.

Human Experimentation

Nuremberg judges codified the first international code for human research experimentation in the wake of the Second World War.[1] But with its strong association with Nazi crimes, the Nuremberg Code seemed irrelevant to most American doctors, who felt that their own practices were in no way comparable to those of Nazi criminals. The revealing of highly questionable research experiments throughout the late 1960s and 1970s put the question of subject consent back at the core of public debates and created a momentum for the regulation of scientists' research activities.

Initial moves to publicise malpractices in medical research came from within the scientific community itself. In 1966, Henry Beecher, a Harvard anaesthesiology professor, published an article on 'Ethics in clinical research', which exposed the extent to which top medical institutions and practitioners in the United States ignored principles of subject consent.[2] Several experiments were of particular concern. One of these took place between the 1950s and the 1970s at the Willowbrook facility, an institution for the people with an intellectual disability on Staten Island. A research team led by Dr Saul Krugman conducted a series of research experiments that included feeding the hepatitis virus to sixty healthy children in order to observe the course of the illness. The experiments were, in fact, well known – the Krugman team published many articles fully describing the protocol, and even

---

[1] The Nuremberg Code was adopted in 1947 following the so-called Doctors' Trial of SS physician Karl Brandt and twenty-two other Nazi doctors in Nuremberg.
[2] See the full account in Beecher 1966.

after Beecher's article, the research went on. Henry Beecher, for his part, essentially called for the medical profession to regulate itself, suggesting the creation of a collective mechanism whereby in order to be published, articles would have to include information on how the consent of the research subjects was obtained. In July 1966, the US Department of Health and Human Services issued guidelines proposing the creation of a peer-review process of all research projects through the newly set-up Institutional Review Boards (IRBs). This new mechanism amounted, however, to an insider's review process, with scientists examining the procedures of other scientists.[3]

Another federally sponsored research project provoked indignation when revealed to the public in the 1970s. The experiment, which was conducted between the mid-1930s and the early 1970s at Tuskegee in Alabama, consisted of leaving poor black men untreated for syphilis in order to study the effects of the disease in advanced stages. Doctors pursued the experiment even after the discovery in 1945 that penicillin could cure the disease. Most questionably, they never informed the research subjects that they were part of a research project that forbade treatment.[4]

In both of these instances, researchers defended their research by arguing that they were conducting 'natural experiments'. In the Tuskegee case, before the discovery that penicillin could cure the disease, doctors claimed that a poor and medically unserved population would in any case never receive the only therapy that existed – a complicated, lengthy, somewhat dangerous, and not altogether effective treatment against syphilis. Since the subjects were not going to obtain treatment anyway, so the researchers claimed, there was no reason to miss the opportunity to trace the effects of their infections. After the effectiveness of penicillin was discovered, the researchers argued that it would be a mistake to abandon the study at this stage, as there would never again be a similar opportunity to observe long-term effects of untreated syphilis. The Krugman team at Willowbrook invoked similar arguments. It too was conducting a natural experiment. Due to poor hygienic conditions, hepatitis was endemic in the facility and new residents would in all likelihood contract the virus within weeks after their arrival.

---

[3] Rothman 1991, p. 17; Fox and Swazey 2008, pp. 34–5.
[4] Fox and Swazey 2008, pp. 46–7.

In both Tuskegee and Willowbrook, researchers insisted that their protocols were ethical and that they were only passive observers of a natural phenomenon.[5] In July 1972, the revealing of the Tuskegee study in *The New York Times* provoked public indignation, in a context of heightened concern about social and racial forms of discriminations.[6] The US government was put in a position where they had to respond, which they did through the creation of the Tuskegee Study Ad Hoc Advisory Panel, and the eventual termination of the Tuskegee study within a month.[7]

Organ Transplantation and the Definition of Life and Death

At the same time, controversies surrounding kidney transplantations, but even more so heart transplantations, also brought the limited relevance of existing ethical solutions to public attention. In December 1967, Dr Christian Barnard, a South African cardiac surgeon, performed the first heart transplant surgery at Groote Schuur Hospital, Cape Town. In the following months, a number of surgeons performed heart transplants throughout the world, raising unprecedented media attention. Dr Christian Barnard and his fellow colleagues communicated directly with the press about their results, often competing for celebrity.[8] But heart transplants provoked major debates, both in the medical profession and in the media.[9] First, a discussion emerged on conflicts of interest which could potentially arise between physicians and patients.[10] Would physicians be willing to do everything possible to save a patient already seriously injured or ill, when their heart could contribute to another person's life? Medical practitioners began to discuss this dilemma in scientific journals, bringing to light the way organ transplants in fact invested doctors with new roles, such as that of adjudicating between protecting the potential interest of a donor and the urgent need of a colleague for an

---

[5] Rothman 1982. [6] Heller 1972. [7] Fox and Swazey 2008, pp. 46–8.
[8] *Time* made Dr Barnard's 'transplanted heart' its front page story. See 'The transplanted heart' 1967.
[9] In February 1968, a special episode of the BBC's *Tomorrow's World* programme called 'Barnard Faces His Critics', and with Dr Barnard present himself, was broadcast. For an account of the episode and the way it made medicine a mediatised issue, see Nathoo 2017.
[10] Rothman 1991, p. 158.

organ to save a patient's life.[11] Second, the question of how to choose the few individuals who would be able to benefit from the procedure was central, triggering debates on resource allocation. And third, organ transplants raised new issues concerning the definition of death. Because such transplants had to be performed with the use of beating hearts, criteria for the moment of death of the donor had to be established. In 1968, a group of Harvard physicians led by Henry Beecher, which became known as the brain death committee, argued in a report that irreversible coma was to become a new criterion for death, and preserved the exclusive prerogative of defining death for doctors.[12] Despite benefiting from broad support within the medical community, the report immediately raised public protests: weren't physicians just concerned with making organs available for transplants? The media widely publicised the issue and asked the crucial question of when the death of a patient should be declared.[13] Such debates increased the public's pleas for greater oversight of decisions taken within the medical profession, and physicians' sentiment that they needed to protect themselves against such intrusion.

Life-and-death issues surfaced again in 1976 before courts, when the Quinlan case exposed conflicts between the claims of physicians and those of a patient's family members over the decision to withhold life support. In April 1975, Karen Ann Quinlan, an American woman then aged twenty-one, lost consciousness after drinking alcohol and taking tranquillisers at a party. While she was unconscious, an extended episode of respiratory failure caused irreversible damage to her brain and resulted in her entering a persistent vegetative state. Her parents requested that her ventilator be turned off, while doctors, afraid of legal prosecution, refused to so. The Quinlans initiated a litigation strategy – further destabilising established notions of scientists' jurisdiction through a judicialisation of the debate – and their request was eventually upheld upon appeal in a 1976 decision of the New Jersey Supreme Court.[14] In the context of the rise of civil rights movements in the 1970s, the media craved such controversies. The case, which

[11] See, for instance, Shillito 1969 for a sense of the discussion amongst scientists on the new dilemmas they encountered.
[12] Ad Hoc Committee of the Harvard Medical School to Examine the Definition of Brain Death 1968.
[13] See, for instance, 'Surgical showbiz' 1968; 'We climbed Everest' 1968.
[14] Decision re *Quinlan*, 70 N.J. 10, 355 A.2d 647, 31 March 1976.

attracted unprecedented attention in the media, continued to reveal to the public that decisions on life and death could not be guided by medical professional norms alone.[15]

Gene Splicing Experiments and Scientists' Attempts at Self-Regulation

Debates on genetic engineering also triggered debates on the need to better control scientists' activities. In the early 1970s, molecular biologists discovered that they could slice and combine genetic material from multiple sources, thereby creating DNA sequences in the laboratory that did not naturally exist. Molecular cloning and recombinant DNA (rDNA; DNA formed by recombination) opened avenues in genetics that offered revolutionary opportunities in medicine, agriculture and industry. But debates arose when some scientists responsible for developing the technology recognised the risks involved in the unregulated proliferation of hybrid organisms. Paul Berg, a biochemist who himself conducted research on hybrid molecules and used techniques which involved the use of bacterial viruses to carry foreign DNA into cells in order to make the cells adopt the DNA, became aware of the hazard this might cause both to laboratory workers and to the public.[16] Together with other colleagues, Berg denounced his experiments. But other scientists continued with their research, and a debate soon surfaced within the scientific community. In this context, scientists grew increasingly concerned that if this internal debate was made public, their activities would become subject to greater public control. According to Berg, 'scientists feared that a public debate would place crippling restrictions on molecular biology'.[17]

In January 1973 and in 1975, Paul Berg organised two conferences at the Asilomar Conference Center (California) in order to discuss the laboratory hazards of working with rDNA. The first conference was more of a scientific meeting to discuss the risks of working with recombinant viruses and gene splicing experiments. Asilomar II gathered 150 scientists in order to discuss the risks of transferring genetic material across species. Crucially, scientists kept framing discussions as an issue

---

[15] See, for instance, Clark 1975; Seligmann 1976.   [16] Evans 2002, pp. 95–6.
[17] Berg 2008, p. 291.

of risk, rather than an ethical one. Debates focused on the efficiency of means for forwarding certain ends and the risks involved in the techniques they intended to use. They carefully avoided opening discussions on whether genetic engineering as a practice was right or wrong. After much debate, participants agreed to a set of restrictions. By taking a proactive approach to the management of unknown risks, participants in Asilomar II could also boast of having adopted a 'model approach' to proactive self-censorship.[18] Yet self-regulation was very strategic. Sydney Brenner, a South African biologist who participated to the conference, 'repeatedly warned of the consequences of doing nothing, predicting that such apparently self-serving behaviour would be publicly condemned and that government interference or even legislation would follow'.[19] Scientific autonomy was the motive driving self-regulation and the discourse on 'social responsibility' at Asilomar. Senator Edward Kennedy, whose role in promoting a better regulation of scientific practices will be detailed in the following section, commented that 'scientists were making public policy' and that 'they were making it in private'.[20]

Public controversies surrounding human experimentation, debates on the allocation of access to scarce medical technologies, and scientific breakthroughs on genetic manipulation constituted the context in which criticisms on the power of clinical decision-making emerged. A handful of disquieted scientists, US citizens alerted by the media, and vocal religious figures – as will be examined in the next section – deemed that scientists should not be left alone any longer to decide on ethical decisions in medicine and science. These scientific breakthroughs and the associated protests they triggered provided the context that made the emergence of a new type of professionals – the expert bioethicists we are concerned with here – possible.

Renegotiating Governance Arrangements: Regulating Scientists' Practices?

Scientists, at their end, were anxious about internal and external claims that their activities should be better regulated. Isolated but active politicians started to call for increased control of their activities. In

---

[18] Evans 2002, pp. 97–8; Krimsky 2005, p. 313.   [19] Cited in Berg 2008, p. 290.
[20] Cited in Evans 2002, p. 97.

1968, Senator Walter Mondale, a member of the Democratic Party, proposed the creation of a government commission to explore heart transplantation and genetic engineering, in which not only doctors and biomedical researchers, but also people from theological, legal, sociological and psychological backgrounds would be represented.[21] Scientists expressed their disquiet. Those who testified before Mondale's Senate subcommittee were largely hostile to the idea.[22] One medical professor commented, 'If you are thinking of theologians, lawyers, philosophers and others to give some direction ... I cannot see how they could help ... the fellow who holds the apple can peel it best.'[23] Another transplant surgeon argued that if such a commission was established, 'physicians should predominate in its membership', making it clear that there are areas in the development of medicine 'where a certain amount of boldness is necessary for success' and doubting that 'committees have established a reputation for courage and boldness'.[24] Scientists protested against the idea that they were facing new ethical dilemmas and, most vehemently, against any form of external interference with their professional activities.

Although Mondale's efforts fell through in 1968, he renewed his attempts in the following years. In the wake of the revelations about the Tuskegee syphilis study, he reintroduced several bills in Congress. He then worked together with Senator Edward Kennedy (the youngest brother of the Kennedy family) to push for some form of regulation of scientific activity. Between February and April 1973 Kennedy held hearings on the Tuskegee study, experimentations with prisoners, children and poor women, and other issues related to biomedical research. The Tuskegee experiment was at the core of discussions, which eventually led to the creation of the National Commission for the Protection of Human Subjects of Biomedical and Behavioural Research in 1973 and the enactment of the National Research Act of 1974. During the legislative debate over the creation of the National Commission, divergent views were expressed, with some in favour of a more permanent and regulatory body, and others – taking the same position as scientists – in favour of an advisory commission. Senator Kennedy vigorously defended the view that physicians must be subject to external oversight

---

[21] S. J. Res 145, 90th Congress (1968). Joint Resolution to Provide for a Study and Evaluation of Scientific Research in Medicine in the United States.
[22] Jonsen 1998, pp. 91–3.   [23] Cited in Jonsen 1998, p. 93.
[24] Cited in Jonsen 1998, p. 91.

in order to avoid dangerous practices happening again.[25] By that time scientists had also realised that some sort of oversight of their practices was going to occur. For instance, Robert Edwards, who researched human fertilisation, admitted that biologists 'must invent a method of taking council of mankind' or 'society will thrust its advice on biologists ... in a manner or form seriously hampering to science'.[26] His position was emblematic of scientists' concerns at the time: some form of oversight had to be consented to, in order to prevent broader and fiercer opposition from the public. But for scientists, the purpose of a bioethics commission consisted, in effect, in ensuring citizens' acceptance of new scientific developments. For instance, William French Anderson, a US physician who was a pioneer of genetic therapy, explained that his ideal form of advisory input from the public was one in which the public 'quickly adjusted itself' to new procedures.[27] A compromise was struck in favour of the creation of an advisory commission, provided that the Department of Health, Education and Welfare published regulations for all research funded by the National Institutes of Health (NIH).

Once in place, the 1973 National Commission was charged with identifying basic ethical principles for research involving human subjects.[28] Its composition foreshadowed the make-up of today's ethics committees: it included specialists from a wide array of disciplines, such as medicine, law, ethics, theology, biology, physics and the social sciences, but no civil society representative.[29] At the time when the National Commission was set up, a group of scholars at Georgetown University was working on a principle-based approach to ethical problems, which we now know as principlism. The National Commission hired its staff mainly amongst the Georgetown academics, and produced its Ethical Principles and Guidelines for the Protection of Human Subjects of Research, eventually published in 1979 as the Belmont Report. The guidelines developed three basic principles, which formalised principlism as a doctrine: (1) respect for persons: the requirement to acknowledge autonomy and the requirement to protect those with diminished autonomy; (2) beneficence: the obligation to maximise benefits and minimise harm; (3) justice: assuring the fair distribution

---

[25] See Evans 2012, p. 40; Jonsen 1998, pp. 95–8.
[26] Edwards and Sharpe 1971, p. 90.   [27] Anderson 1971, p. 120.
[28] Evans 2002, p. 83.   [29] Evans 2012, p. 40.

of benefits.[30] Principlism, an essentially utilitarian framework formulated by the Georgetown academics, met the needs of policymakers for a clear and simple statement of the ethical basis for regulation and research. The National Commission needed to create principles which could be 'made into fairly calculable rules', universally applicable to all recipients of research grants, regardless of the type of research conducted.[31] Lopez also argues that principlism was quickly taken on board by all relevant actors because 'it was transparent, formally rational and bureaucratically friendly, value free and apparently impartial'.[32] Given that several theologians participated in the National Commission, it is not obvious why they supported this form of rationalist argumentation. For Evans, a faction of theologians, including James Childress, one of the authors of the Belmont Report, 'believed in universally accessible ethics, stated in secular language, that did not have to return each time to the well of theological discourse for discernment'.[33] With its formal style of argumentation, principlism is strongly connected to the emergence of bioethics as a profession. The doctrine benefited from strong governmental support and progressively became the dominant creed amongst bioethicists.

From that moment on all IRBs in academic institutions that received federal funding had to comply with these principles. Given that journals would not normally publish research not formerly reviewed by IRBs, all research projects in fact started to apply those standards. According to Evans, 'this was a huge resource given to the new profession of bioethics in its competition with other professions'.[34] By requiring all recipients of federal funding to establish IRBs for monitoring research protocols and risk–benefit ratios, a nationwide demand for non-medical professional ethical expertise was generated. In a swift phenomenon of 'ethics creep', the principles outlined in the Belmont Report were soon applied to other areas of human medicine and science, becoming the standard approach to evaluating ethical issues arising in all areas of scientific development.[35]

By the 1980s, the US government heavily relied on expert bioethicists as a new category of specialists. Thus, while the invention of 'bioethics' as a new set of *concerns* with the ethics of medicine and scientific

---

[30] National Commission for the Protection of Human Subjects of Biomedical and Behavioral Research 1978/1979.
[31] Evans 2002, p. 85.   [32] Lopez 2004, p. 889.   [33] Evans 2002, p. 87.
[34] Evans 2002, p. 89.   [35] Bosk 1999; Evans 1991, pp. 89–90.

practices was born out by anxiety on the part of a handful of scientists, engaged politicians and critical citizens that scientists should not be left to themselves to decide what kind of research to conduct and what scientific developments to promote, its tangible manifestation took the form of a new *expert discourse*. Bioethicists, a new-fangled category of professionals, through their involvement in public decisions on science, pushed the boundaries of scientific expertise away from questions now defined as ethical or bioethical. At the same time, however, they provided scientists with a *friendly form of control on their activities* and protected them from any form of public oversight.

The Making of Expert Bioethicists

The creation of bioethics bodies was indeed intertwined with the fabric of a new type of expertise – which we might call ethical or bioethical expertise – which complements, and on some occasions replaces, the expertise of scientists and doctors. The emergence of the notion of ethical expertise was made possible by the appearance of specialised academic programmes in ethics and bioethics. From the 1970s on in the United States, and a decade later in Europe, a number of universities created new degrees in applied ethics, ethics and bioethics, contributing to establishing and legitimising the notion of an autonomous field of knowledge focused on the study of ethical problems arising in relation to medicine and the life sciences. Scholars working in the field soon created their own scientific journals, professional associations and terminology, successfully delineating the contours of a new discipline. The emergence of bioethics was strongly enmeshed with policy, with scholars circulating between the two spheres, and public funding shaping which types of bioethical enquiry would become mainstream.

Because resources were often located within academic departments of medicine, centres and institutes in bioethics were initially developed there.[36] Those who helped set up these programmes in medical departments were either theologians, religious physicians or scientists. Paul Ramsey, a Catholic theologian from Princeton University who became a leading 'bioethicist', felt that medicine could not be left to its own devices.[37] Preoccupied with scientists' activities in the field of genetic engineering in particular, Ramsey argued that it was impossible to

[36] Bosk 1999. [37] Rothman 1991.

believe 'that either the codes of medical ethics or the physicians who have undertaken to comment on them ... will suffice to withstand the omnivorous appetite of scientific research ... that has momentum and a life of its own'.[38] In the 1960s 'the only resources were theological or those drawn from the traditions of medicine, themselves heavily shaped by religion'.[39] Scholars attracted to medical-ethical issues were, for the most part, trained theologians or doctors affiliated to a Catholic or Protestant Church. A few philosophers and social scientists were also drawn into medical issues, shocked by revelations of unethical practices in human experimentation. But, as Thomasma put it, 'ethics was not where the action was in philosophy ... and applied philosophy was the lowest possible kind of philosophy in the hierarchy of the department'.[40] Philosophers were also critical of the rise of principlism as a dominant bioethics doctrine. Cultural relativism had established itself as a dominant ontological posture in philosophy departments, and philosophers looked suspiciously at principlism, a doctrine meant to apply universally.[41] Thus, although influenced by religious ethics, bioethics as a discipline developed neither in theology nor in philosophy departments; it advanced within the institutional structure and with the institutional resources of academic medicine.

From the late 1960s on, medical schools started including bioethics in their curricula. The Pennsylvania State University Medical Center created the first Department of Medical Humanities with a faculty weighted towards medical ethics. On the West Coast of the United States, bioethics was advanced by the writings and teachings of Albert Jonsen at the University of San Francisco and the University of California, San Francisco (UCSF). Albert Jonsen, who was a Catholic priest, received a doctorate in religious studies from Yale in 1967. He became president of the University of San Francisco two years later, and was asked to establish a programme in medical ethics at UCSF. The University of Chicago also started a training programme for clinical bioethicists, and with funding from the Kennedy Foundation, the Harvard School of Public Health also created a small medical ethics programme in 1972.

An important step in the professionalisation of bioethics took place in 1969, when Daniel Callahan, a Catholic layman with a PhD in

---

[38] Cited in Rothman 1991, p. 96.   [39] Callahan 1990, p. 2.
[40] Thomasma 2002, p. 339.   [41] Bosk 1999.

philosophy, together with Willard Gaylin, a psychiatrist, created the Hastings Center in New York. Daniel Callahan had long been interested in moral issues regarding medicine, advocating for greater reflection on doctors' practices and the need to involve other professions in the evaluation of medical practices. He was at that time conducting research on population control and family planning, and succeeded in mobilising the Rockefeller Foundation, which was also interested in the establishment of family planning units for university research and teaching in a number of US academic institutions, and provided the Hastings Center with significant funding.[42] As the first autonomous bioethics institution, the Hastings Center played an instrumental role in establishing bioethics as an autonomous discipline. In particular, it published the field's first journal, the *Hastings Center Report*, as well as the *Hastings Centre Studies* – the inaugural issue of which included an essay from Daniel Callahan himself, entitled 'Bioethics as a discipline'.[43] The Hastings Center promoted the adoption of medical ethics in the curricula of schools of medicine, but was itself not attached to any department of medicine, or law, and helped sustain an appearance of the field's independence. In Callahan's words, bioethics was a field that its practitioners 'were more or less inventing ... as they went along'.[44]

In 1971, André Hellegers, a Dutch obstetrician and Jesuit priest, together with his colleagues inaugurated another institute at Georgetown that would apply moral philosophy to medical dilemmas: the Joseph and Rose Kennedy Center for the Study of Human Reproduction and Bioethics (now known as the Kennedy Institute of Ethics). The Kennedy Institute of Ethics was initially funded by a grant from the Kennedy Foundation, headed by Senator Edward Kennedy, who was at the time pleading for better control of medical research in the Senate, bringing to light the enmeshment between policy debates and the emergence of bioethics as an autonomous field of study within universities.[45] André Hellegers formalised the use of the term 'bioethics'

---

[42] See website of the Rockefeller Foundation: www.rockefellerfoundation.org/about-us/our-history.
[43] Callahan 1973.   [44] Callahan 1973, p. 68.
[45] The Kennedy family had a strong preoccupation with biological research on people with an intellectual disability (Joseph and Rose Kennedy had a daughter born with an intellectual disability), and were convinced by Hellegers to invest some of their funds in the creation of the Institute for Bioethics.

'to designate the focused area of enquiry that became an academic field of learning and a movement regarding public policy and the life sciences'.[46] The Institute developed the National Reference Center for Bioethics Literature, which became the best library resource in the field. One of the first Kennedy Institute scholars, Warren Reich, a Catholic theologian, also put together the *Encyclopaedia of Bioethics*, which was published in 1978 and became a major resource for the discipline.[47] A Protestant scholar with a PhD in 'Christian Ethics', Leroy Walters, started an annual *Bibliography of Bioethics* and developed BioethicsLine, an online computer database. Tom Beauchamp and James Childress, both scholars at the Kennedy Institute, published their seminal book, *Principles of Bioethics*, in 1979, which promoted principlism as a doctrine.[48] Tom Beauchamp had in fact already laid out these principles when appointed to work for the 1973 National Commission for the Protection of Human Subjects of Biomedical and Behavioural Research, where he wrote the bulk of what became known as the 1979 Belmont Report. The shaping of bioethics was strongly enmeshed with public policymaking, with scholars acting in different roles in both spheres, and public funding shaping the edge of bioethics as a field of enquiry. High-profile individuals such as the Kennedys, for personal motives, or foundations such as the Rockefeller Foundation, the Russell Sage Foundation, the Ford Foundation and others, played a central role in funding the creation of bioethics departments.[49] The National Endowment for the Humanities (NEH), a grant-making agency of the US government dedicated to supporting research, education and public programmes in the humanities, was also a major supporter of bioethics as an academic discipline, evidencing the US government's support for making bioethics an independent field of enquiry. When the US government set up the 1974 Commission for the Study of the Protection of Human Subjects of Biomedical and Behavioural Research, it in turn heavily relied on the new 'bioethicists' who had contributed to establishing the field. Albert Jonsen, who created the bioethics programme at UCSF, was appointed to the National Commission in 1974, and selected as a member of the first NIH committee to examine the ethical, legal and social aspects of a developing medical technology, the implantable artificial heart. Tom Beauchamp,

---

[46] Reich 1994, p. 319.　　[47] Fox and Swazey 2008, p. 39.
[48] Now in its eighth edition; Beauchamp and Childress 2019.　　[49] Levine 2007.

a prominent scholar from the Kennedy Institute, joined the staff of the National Commission for the Protection of Human Subjects of Biomedical and Behavioural Research in 1975, where he wrote the bulk of the Belmont Report.[50]

During the 1970s and 1980s, bioethics became part of the curriculum of most schools of medicine, and autonomous bioethics institutes were also set in place. Thus, bioethics increasingly shaped its contours as that of an autonomous discipline, in turn legitimising the notion of a new form of expertise in moral analysis. But the notion of bioethics was contested. Theologians, doctors and philosophers debated the content of bioethics as a new field of academic enquiry. Principlism, however, established itself as the dominant doctrine, because it benefited from clear political backing. Making a mainstream version of bioethics not only delegitimised alternative voices within the expert sphere, but it also sidelined claims by lay patients and consumers that they should be permitted to participate in such debates.

This move, initiated in the US context, soon spread out to Europe. The Hastings Center and the Kennedy Institute of Ethics at Georgetown University have welcomed a number of researchers and scientists from Europe and, from the 1990s on, the developing world. The Hastings Center through its Eastern European Programme has boosted the training of scholars and professionals to enter the fields of medical ethics or bioethics. At the Kennedy Institute, courses essentially promoted Beauchamp and Childress's version of principlism and acted as a central mechanism of diffusion of the doctrine.[51] Dr Francesc Abel, who came from Spain to study medicine with André Hellegers at the Kennedy Institute, went back to Barcelona and set up the Borja Institute, the first bioethics institute in Europe.[52] In 1986, Abel also created the European Association of Centres of Medical Ethics, which played an important role in institutionalising the field in Europe. The Hastings Center also promoted international networks of scholars in the field, sponsoring the first International Conference on Teaching Medical Ethics.[53] Thus, US developments shaped the contours of

---

[50] Faculty profile of Tom Beauchamp on the website of Georgetown University: https://gufaculty360.georgetown.edu/s/contact/00336000014RlsjAAC/tom-beauchamp.
[51] Fox and Swazey, 2008, p. 222.   [52] Harvey, 2013, p. 49.
[53] Fox and Swazey 2008, pp. 223–4.

bioethics as a discipline and also influenced what was going to take place in Europe.

Crossing the Atlantic

Developments in Europe caught up about a decade later, with the creation of national commissions of ethics experts, appointed by national governments, in Western European countries. Today all European governments have included ethical analysis in public decision-making concerning medicine and the life sciences. US developments have widely influenced European bioethics: principlism, and utilitarian principles more generally, were widely 'imported' from one side of the Atlantic to the other and became part of national debates on bioethics in most European country settings. Of course, the creation of national ethics committees has also been influenced by the historical specificities and political circumstances of different domestic contexts. Specific factors also shape what is defined as 'bioethical' in different times and places. But common trends are decipherable; as in the US case, public mechanisms of bioethical analysis emerged, essentially, out of a concern to *make possible* the advancement of scientific and technological advances, rather than prevent them.

In France President François Mitterrand established the first group to provide ethical assistance to policy in Europe, the *Comité Consultatif National d'Ethique* (CCNE), in 1983. The legal cases on the right to die or publicised instances of medical experimentations on humans of the kind that occurred in the United States had no precedent in France. Discussions on some form of societal oversight over medical and scientific practices emerged, essentially, in relation to debates on reproductive medicine. President Giscard d'Estaing had already, after the first birth from in vitro fertilisation (IVF) in the UK in 1978, commissioned a report on the consequences of biological advances on family structure, gender relations and demographic composition. The report suggested, for the first time, that the development of life sciences should be the object of reflection by a body composed not only of scientists 'but also of persons with various competencies'.[54] Following the birth of the first French *bébé éprouvette* (test-tube baby), Amandine, in 1982, advances in assisted reproductive technology (ART) received intense

---

[54] Gros et al. 1979, p. 280.

national media coverage.⁵⁵ The birth of Amandine was the object of widespread public debate about the moral, philosophical and legal dilemmas posed by the new technologies. It was in this context that President François Mitterrand decided to act on the report commissioned by his predecessor and establish the *CCNE* in 1983. The *CCNE* comprises government-nominated experts overwhelmingly from the medical profession, reflecting a general aversion, in France more even than anywhere else, to taking ethical reflection on medicine and science away from the professional remit of doctors.⁵⁶ The way bioethics was taught in French universities brings evidence of this. Few departments carried the name 'bioethics', and when courses were developed it was always within medical schools. In 1984, Lille Catholic University created the first centre for the study of medical ethics in France. In 1992, the Faculty of Medicine of Necker-Enfants Malades set up a Masters' Programme in Medical and Biological Ethics. In the mid-1990s, two professors also initiated a teaching programme in medical ethics at the Faculty of Medicine at Aix-Marseille. One of them, Jean-François Mattei, is a physician and former minister of health who also worked as an expert for the *CCNE*. Bioethics struggled to assert itself as an autonomous discipline; doctors and other scientists essentially kept control over the study of ethical problems arising from their work, and when interdisciplinarity was included in the national ethics body, it came under the form of the convening of a handful of religious representatives (5 out of 39 *CCNE* members).⁵⁷

The Swedish government soon after created the Swedish National Council on Medical Ethics in 1985. Denmark set up its own council of ethics in 1987, Luxembourg its *Commission Consultative Nationale d'Ethique* in 1988 and Norway its National Committee for Medical and Health Research Ethics in 1990. Also, in 1990, Italy created its National Bioethics Committee. Other European countries followed the move, with the UK creating the Nuffield Council on Bioethics in 1991, and Belgium setting up its own Advisory Committee on Bioethics in 1993.

In the UK, US developments provided a stimulus for change through the role of scholars who had visited US universities. In the late 1970s the British Medical Association considered that outside involvement in

---

⁵⁵ See, for instance, United Press International 1982. ⁵⁶ Guerrier 2006, p. 503.
⁵⁷ Fox and Swazey 2008, pp. 239–42.

doctors' professional practices would 'endanger research, increase waiting-lists and threaten the health and morale of doctors'.[58] Professionalised bioethics was dismissed as an American invention, and had few sympathetic advocates. Medical schools began integrating courses on medical ethics from the late 1970s onwards, but doctors were seen as solely responsible for teaching the subject. Ian Kennedy, a lawyer and lecturer of jurisprudence at University College London who conducted research in the United States, was, however, instrumental in importing American ideas about bioethics into the UK. He became the highest-profile advocate of some form of external oversight over doctors' performance, lamenting that 'the formal teaching of medical ethics is a desultory exercise'. Involving non-doctors in courses was the only way, from his perspective, to drag medical schools 'out of their hermetically sealed cocoons'.[59] In reaction to his calls, several programmes started to include a growing number of lawyers or philosophers in medical ethics teaching. Kennedy eventually established the Centre for Medical Law and Ethics at Kings College in 1979. His arguments reached a broad audience through a series of lectures aired by the BBC (British Broadcasting Corporation), provocatively entitled *Unmasking Medicine*.[60] These demands, although arising from a different set of concerns, resonated with the Thatcher government's anxieties over human fertilisation and embryology. After the birth of Louise Brown, the first IVF baby, in 1978, the media and Conservative politicians started to call for a public inquiry into IVF, as well as hESC research. In 1982, the Thatcher government appointed Mary Warnock, a fellow in philosophy at Oxford University, to chair the inquiry. The Warnock Commission advocated the utilitarian approach that prevailed in the United States, arguing that 'the criterion of right and wrong must be the balance of pleasure over pain'.[61] The key proposal of the Commission involved establishing a monitoring body, chaired by a layperson, composed of both professionals and non-professionals from a variety of backgrounds to ensure the increased empowerment of public stakeholders in the governance of such practices. But both Kennedy and Warnock argued that public accountability would protect, rather than impede research, while allowing scientists to offload

---

[58] Anon. 1977, p. 1238. [59] Kennedy 1980, p. 715.
[60] Wilson 2014, pp. 105–7. See also BBC website for a presentation of the talks from Ian Kennedy: www.bbc.co.uk/programmes/p00h2dmp.
[61] Warnock 1985, p. 516.

a portion of the ethical burden.[62] Despite these calls, Conservative politicians were reluctant to remain ensnared by divisive issues such as IVF, embryo research and gene therapy, and eventually favoured the creation of an independent body.[63] The decision was taken, therefore, to establish a free-standing council which could examine the ethical issues raised by research advances. It was Sir David Weatherhall, a clinical geneticist at the University of Oxford interested in ethical issues, who approached the chairman of the Nuffield Foundation to ask whether it would establish a bioethics body – which we now know as the Nuffield Council on Bioethics.[64] By then, bioethics had also gained legitimacy as an autonomous discipline. Advocates of a 'multidisciplinary teaching' of bioethics played a key role in promoting the creation of dedicated bioethics centres from the late 1980s on, which were instrumental, as had been the case in the United States, in legitimising the idea that bioethics was becoming an independent discipline. This move was also indirectly facilitated by the Conservative government's demands that universities be more responsive to the needs of the job market and make themselves more self-sufficient. A number of philosophers, lawyers and other social scientists were pushed to engage with more practical issues, such as bioethics, in order to stand a better chance of getting funding and meeting demands that research had to be of obvious practical relevance.[65]

Germany caught up with the creation of its *Nationaler Ethikrat* in 2001 (now called *Deutscher Ethikrat*), with Austria and Switzerland creating their own bioethics commissions the same year. In Germany, the memory of Nazism has permeated every discussion of biotechnology and genetics. Germans have been particularly sensitive to reprogenetic technologies, such as cloning, preimplantation genetic diagnosis (PGD) and germ line engineering, which they saw as technologies that bore the potential of selecting individuals with 'superior' genotypes. In this context, Germany has enacted some of the strictest policies in the world on euthanasia, surrogate motherhood, IVF, experimentation with human subjects, and the manipulation of nascent human life. Germany's 1991 Embryo Protection Act explicitly made ex vivo embryos protected subjects, and also banned surrogacy, egg donation,

---

[62] Wilson 2014, pp. 158–9, 227; See also Warnock 1988.
[63] Lock 1990, p. 1149.   [64] Nuffield Council on Bioethics 2000, p. 3.
[65] Wilson 2014, pp. 196–8.

embryo transfer, germ line manipulation, both non-therapeutic and therapeutic human cloning, and the creation of 'surplus' embryos for research.[66] The law went largely unchallenged until the late 1990s, but became the object of public debate when some scientists challenged it for being too restrictive. In 1996, a gynaecologist sought to conduct PGD on a patient. In the following years, the medical community, supported by a number of policymakers, battled to make PGD legal, arguing that it could help high-risk couples to have healthy children. A counter coalition, composed of disability rights groups, religious representatives, pro-life advocates and feminists, feared that PGD would instead be used to 'select babies' and that its legal acceptance would also signal to people with disabilities that they are not welcomed.[67] Andrea Fischer, then health minister, convened a ministry-level interdisciplinary ethics advisory board and initiated a public symposium to explore the topic, as well as that of hESC research, as scientists started to request to import embryonic stem cells from abroad.[68] The tenants of a strict legislative framework evoked the memory of Nazism, and argued that one should not distinguish between 'life worth living' and 'life not worth living'.[69] These debates were echoed in universities, where some German scholars had found themselves under pressure because they were perceived as teaching utilitarian bioethics principles imported from the United States.[70] It was in this context that Chancellor Schroeder, who was favourable to embryo research, created the *National Ethikrat*, perceived as 'the Chancellor's instrument to secure public consent to ready-made political decisions'.[71] The Council's composition indeed favoured 'techno-optimist' experts from philosophy, the medical research community and the law.[72] Since its inception, the *National Ethikrat* has weighed in on controversial issues, generally voicing support for relaxing restrictive measures. The German bioethics council was created in a specific domestic context, and out of a perceived need on the part of policymakers to *facilitate scientific advances* perceived as controversial by some segments of the society.

[66] Brown 2004; Wikler and Barondess 1993.
[67] For a detailed account of the controversy see Braun 2005.
[68] In 2001 the German Research Foundation requested to import embryonic stem cells from abroad; see Krones 2006.
[69] Bundesministerium für Gesundheit 2000.   [70] Singer 1991.
[71] Braun and Kropp 2010, p. 774.   [72] Braun 2005, p. 47.

Whereas the creation of ethics committees was initially a US, and then Western European phenomenon, such advisory bodies exist more or less everywhere today. Most Central and Eastern European countries created their own national ethics committees throughout the 1990s. Slovenia was exceptionally early in setting up its National Medical Ethics Committee in 1977; other countries caught up from the 1990s onwards: Lithuania in 1995, Poland and the Czech Republic in 1997, Estonia and Latvia in 1998, and Croatia and the Slovak Republic in 2004. In August 2000, the Central and East European Association of Bioethics (CEEAB) was also set in place. In Croatia, the University of Rijeka's Faculty of Medicine started a new course entitled 'Hippocratic Oath Today' in 1991. In Estonia, the Faculty of Medicine at the University of Tartu also introduced bioethics as a compulsory discipline for its students in 1991.[73] In Bulgaria, medical schools introduced courses in medical ethics throughout the early 1990s, and since 1996 medical ethics has been taught in all medical colleges.[74]

Policymakers are now mobilising expert bioethicists in an increasingly large number of domestic contexts. Both in the United States and in Europe, scientists' professional remit has been more tightly delineated, and individuals trained as 'bioethicists' have gained jurisdiction to decide on the ethical nature of their activities. This shift is not without setbacks, however. In some national contexts, medical schools still provide a large share of the existing training in ethics, and scientists are over-represented in national bioethics commissions, testifying to the reluctance of doctors and scientists to let go, and auguring the science-friendly role of bioethicists in scientific and technological policymaking.

Bioethics Creep in Domestic and Global Arenas

At the global level, international organisations have started mobilising expert bioethicists as they have become increasingly involved with the governance of scientific and technological developments. The United Nations Educational, Scientific and Cultural Organisation (UNESCO)

---

[73] Glasa 2002.
[74] See ten Have and Gordijn 2014 for a complete overview of national bioethics committees.

has equipped itself with a powerful bureaucratic structure to deal with bioethics. In addition to the creation of its Division on Ethics of Science and Technology in the 1990s, it has set up the International Bioethics Committee (IBC), composed of high-profile experts in the field.[75] It was also in the early 1990s that the European Commission set in place the Group of Advisers on the Ethical Implications of Biotechnology (GAEIB) to issue independent advice strictly on the ethical implications of biotechnology. In 1998, the GAEIB became the European Group on Ethics (EGE) – our object of empirical analysis in the in-depth cases of the book. The World Health Organization (WHO) has also been concerned with several questions defined as 'global bioethics topics' such as organ and tissue transplantation, developments in genomics, the HIV/AIDS epidemic, research with humans and fair access to health services. In order to deal with such issues, it has relied heavily on the mobilisation of existing advisory bioethics committees at the domestic level, setting in place in 2001 the Global Network of WHO Collaborating Centres for Bioethics. The Collaborating Centres are top national centres that research bioethical issues which, according to the WHO, 'represent a valuable resource as an extended and integral arm of WHO's capacity to implement its ethics mandate'.[76] In addition to the separate initiatives of these organisations, the Global Summit of National Bioethics Advisory Bodies, launched for the first time in 1996, at the initiative of the US National Bioethics Advisory Commission and the French *CCNE*, provides 'a platform for exchange of information about on-going work of the national ethics committees'.[77] American bioethicists were key actors in the globalisation of bioethics. Alexander Capron, the former director of the US President's Commission for the Study of Ethical Problems in Medicine and Biomedical and Behavioral Research, initiated the first Global Summit of National Bioethics Committees.[78] International organisations have also massively resorted to US-trained bioethicists as advisors. Daniel Wikler, a professor of ethics who had also served for the US President's Commission, was the first 'staff ethicist' for WHO.

International organisations such as the Council of Europe, UNESCO and WHO, which sometimes acted as staging posts of US dominant

---

[75] Littoz-Monnet 2017. [76] World Health Organisation 2011.
[77] See the website of World Health Organization, The Global Summit of National Bioethics Advisory Bodies, www.who.int/ethics/partnerships/globalsummit/en.
[78] Fox and Swazey 2008, p. 220.

doctrines in bioethics, have actively promoted the creation of bioethics committees beyond the West. The Council of Europe, as well as WHO, have also been active. Ethics committees have been created in Latin America, Philippines, Pakistan, Japan, Singapore, South Korea, Turkey, Russia and Israel. More recently, UNESCO has promoted the creation of such committees in developing countries, such as Colombia, Côte d'Ivoire, El Salvador, Gabon, Ghana, Guinea, Jamaica, Kenya, Chad, Madagascar, Mali, Oman and Togo.[79] Discussions are ongoing concerning the establishment of bioethics committees in Brazil, Kuwait, Morocco, Botswana, Nigeria, Namibia, Costa Rica, Ecuador, Uruguay and Senegal. The UNESCO Ethics Unit also sponsors the development of education and teaching programmes aimed at training the experts appointed as members of the newly created ethics committees in developing countries.[80] Under the spur of the United States, and then international organisations, bioethics has established itself as an expert discourse in domestic and global governance arenas.

The genealogy of bioethical expertise alerts us to various facets of the nature of bioethical expertise: its enmeshment with public decision-making, its ongoing struggle to gain its autonomy from the discipline of medicine and its contested status. The mainstream version of bioethics which emerged from the 1970s is compatible with the 'progress through medical and scientific innovation' narrative of policymakers. Specific doctrines and concepts laid out by bioethicists, such as principlism, make such agendas possible. Mainstream bioethics embodies a particular way of knowing things, which in turn shapes the contours of how new technologies are evaluated and acted upon. Bioethical knowledge is thus embodied within a dominant discourse, and also makes its perpetuation possible. In that sense we observe a process of co-production between knowledge and politics. But the notion of bioethics is contested. A range of actors – groups of citizens, theologians and bioethicists who do not adhere to mainstream doctrines in the field – contest the agenda of bioethics. Policymakers thus need to prevent contestation from within the field of bioethics and from outside. Orchestration, ideational alignment and calibration act as stabilisation strategies which ensure that no counter-narrative develops, as will be examined in the empirical chapters that follow.

[79] UNESCO 2010.   [80] Littoz-Monnet 2017.

4 | *Researching Embryonic Stem Cells*
Bypassing Conflict

This chapter examines the role of the European Group on Ethics (EGE) during the controversial and highly publicised negotiations on the funding of human embryonic stem cell (hESC) research under the EU Framework Programmes (FPs) for Research. Although the EU's competences in the field of embryo research are limited to strictly delineated issues such as patent law and research funding, in practice debates on these specific aspects of biotechnology policy have induced more fundamental discussions on the status of the human embryo and what human life is, with member states, interest groups and civil society actors defending fundamentally irreconcilable positions.

The chapter examines the production and mobilisation of ethical expertise during the political controversies that arose in the context of negotiations on the funding of hESC research under the Sixth Framework Programme (FP6) and the Seventh Framework Programme (FP7). The EGE produced two opinions in the context of these two sets of negotiations. Both in the context of FP6 and of FP7, policy conflict was patent and hard to disentangle. The case of embryo research provides us with an instance of expert mobilisation – and expertise production – in a situation of intense conflict, in which actors framed their positions in moral terms that did not seem to be amenable to any form of compromise or consensual solution.

Both for FP6 and FP7, the mobilisation of ethics experts allowed EU policymakers to manoeuvre through or bypass political discussions, prevent deadlock and ultimately go ahead with research on hESCs, their favoured agenda. The mobilisation of ethical expertise played such functions in policy because the production of ethical expertise took place in iteration with policy itself.

During the negotiations on FP6, the European Commission mobilised ethics experts in an attempt to bypass the political conflict that had surfaced. By establishing closer institutional links between the EGE and the Commission, EU policymakers were able to *orchestrate* the EGE's work. But such moves were effortless, because policymakers and experts had worked together and developed common ways of thinking on embryo research. They in fact formulated a common position – common to experts and policymakers alike – that seemed acceptable to all. Shifting the locus of the debate to the expert arena also made the technicalisation of the issue of embryo research possible. Ethics experts approached the issue in a seemingly scientific and technical tone and presented a range of complex intermediary scenarios which shifted the debate away from the 'either/or' positions that had been voiced until then. This, in turn, eased the delineating of a workable policy scenario, which could then be mobilised by EU policymakers as a legitimate end point to make the funding of hESC research possible even in the *absence* of agreement amongst all the actors involved – member states, religious groups, scientists and patient organisations.

During the FP7 negotiations, the mobilisation of ethics experts allowed EU policymakers to manoeuvre conflict in a highly effective way. At a time when the composition of the EGE had changed, EU policymakers carefully orchestrated the EGE's work. By delineating very strictly the mandate of the EGE, the Commission made sure that the principle of hESC research funding would not be reopened to discussion. At the same time, by delegating the definition of the modalities of such research to a 'conservative' expert group, it secured the support of member states opposed to embryo research. Involving ethics experts in policy provided an 'ethics warrant' to more conservative states, by reassuring them that strict standards would be set on the modalities of hESC research. Involving ethics experts in policy allowed policymakers to manoeuvre through the conflict by giving the appearance that the EGE acted as a counterweight to the Commission's pro-research position. In reality, the EGE opinion, because of the dynamics that characterised the process of knowledge production, did not represent any kind of substantial challenge to the Commission's position. The thrust of the bioethical knowledge produced was stabilised through orchestration, ideational alignment and calibration, and bioethics itself acted as a stabilisation technique to make sure that the EU's agenda would go ahead.

Policy Deadlock on Embryo Research

Embryo research has, from the 1990s on, provoked intense and emotional debates amongst social actors, policymakers, scientists and the industry, polarising EU debates in unprecedented ways. While EU intervention with regard to the regulation of 'green' biotechnologies has been extended from the 1990s on, EU competences in the field of 'red' biotechnologies have been circumscribed to strictly delineated aspects of such policies, such as patenting law and decisions on research funding.[1] The patenting of biotechnological inventions is regulated by a 1998 directive, which excludes from patentability 'uses of human embryos for industrial or commercial purposes',[2] but does not actually give a definition of the human embryo. The European Court of Justice (ECJ) has played a role in asserting the EU's competence in this issue domain. In October 2011, it formulated for the first time a 'European' definition of the embryo in the case *Oliver Brüstel* v. *Greenpeace*, which dealt with the patenting of research conducted on hESCs.[3]

But debates have crystallised, essentially, around the question of the funding of hESC research by the EU. Thus, although EU legislation does not tackle research on embryos or embryonic tissues, the issue has been at the core of the negotiations on EU Framework Programmes. During the negotiations for the FP6 and FP7, two coalitions of actors have organised themselves in order to shape policy.[4] Through the question of funding, more fundamental discussions on whether embryo research should be permitted at all – and on the status of the human embryo – have arisen.

Member states, interest groups and civil society actors have voiced fundamentally irreconcilable policy positions. One coalition, composed of religious groups, conservative Members of the European Parliament (MEPs) and unexpected allies – such as Greenpeace and

---

[1] Hennette-Vauchez 2010. *Green biotechnologies* relates to the use of altered plants or animals, while *red biotechnologies* refers to the use of biological processes, as in the exploitation and manipulation of living organisms or biological systems.

[2] Article 6(2) (c) of Directive 98/44/EC.

[3] Case C34/10, 18 October 2011. Full text of the judgment available at https://eur-lex.europa.eu/legal-content/EN/TXT/HTML/?uri=CELEX:62010CJ0034&from=EN.

[4] Although a small number of projects involving embryonic stem cell research had been funded under FP5, the issue had not given rise to an open and public debate then.

Friends of the Earth – has opposed the funding of hESC research. Religious groups have acted as active lobbyists. Central to their discourse is the concept of human dignity, which they use in order to defend the protection of the embryo. Care for Europe, a Christian NGO claiming to represent the viewpoints of churches and individual Christians across Europe, has, for instance, carried out active advocacy campaigns in EU arenas on issues such as genetic engineering, human cloning and new medical technologies.[5] Comment on Reproductive Ethics (CORE), another Christian pro-life organisation in the UK, has also been active at the EU level. The Commission of the Bishops' Conferences of the European Community (COMECE) acted as another stark opponent of hESC research. The position of COMECE is well laid out in this statement:

> COMECE reiterates that research finds its limits in the inviolable dignity of human life. For this reason – and also in view of the legal situation in several member states – the instrumentalisation of human life, independently of its stage of development, is not acceptable. In the 7th Research Framework Programme research areas are being determined as common priorities through joint financing. It is regrettable that the European Commission did not take into account the fundamental ethical objections regarding research areas such as cloning, human embryo and embryonic stem cell research; areas where there is no consensus about the ethical issues concerned in and among the member states.[6]

Institutionally, these groups have benefited from the support of MEPs from the European People's Party–European Democrats group (EPP-ED). After the Eastern enlargement of the EU, MEPs from Catholic Eastern European states joined forces together with Christian Democrats in their struggle against the funding of embryo research. Amongst EU member states, Germany, Austria, Malta and some Eastern European states have routinely expressed their objection to the funding of hESC research.

The opposing coalition, composed of the Directorate General for Research and Innovation ('DG RESEARCH') within the European Commission, a majority of liberal MEPs and patients' organisations, as well as the scientific community, strongly support the funding of

---

[5] See policy statement, available at https://humanistfederation.eu/radical-religious-lobbies/care-for-europe.
[6] COMECE 2005.

stem cell research. As the unit responsible for the management of the successive FPs, DG RESEARCH has been closely involved in the debate and has defended a pro-hESC research agenda, underlining the great potential of scientific progress based on hESC research.[7] In an attempt to build support for its agenda, DG RESEARCH has backed the activities of patients' organisations, which in general support research advances and the fast transformation of research achievements into clinical applications.[8] The European Federation of Neurological Associations (EFNA), the European Parkinson's Disease Association (EPDA) and the European Genetic Alliances' Network (EGAN) have been amongst the most active associations. Working closely with patients' representatives also made it easier for DG RESEARCH to give an ethical framing to its arguments. It presented embryo research as crucial to save patients' lives, in addition to being an important aspect of the EU's research and economic competitiveness strategy.

Patients' organisations have, for their part, built alliances with industry stakeholders in support of hESC research in an attempt to countervail pro-life campaigners.[9] Patients' organisations have established regular contacts with the European Federation of Pharmaceutical Industries and Associations (EFPIA) and an institutionalised form of work collaboration within the framework of the European Platform for Patients' Organisations, Science and Industry (EPPOSI) platform, which represents both patients and the industry.[10] Hugo Schepens, Secretary-General of EuropaBio, which represents the European biotechnology industry, said that 'research involving all types of human stem cells should be supported under clear conditions', explaining that 'this is important for competitiveness, for patients, for research and for the European bioscience industry'.[11] Finally, the scientific community has also joined the contest, asking for more 'freedom for scientific research' and arguing that stem-cell research is crucial for the development of possible cures for diseases such as Alzheimer's.[12] The European Research Advisory Board (ERAB) has, for instance, actively lobbied in

---

[7] Interviews with EU officials, October 2012.
[8] Interview with an official from Dutch Genetic Alliance of parent and patient organisations, 15 August 2012.
[9] Interview with representative of a patient organisation, 15 August 2012.
[10] Interview with representative of a patient organisation, 15 August 2012.
[11] 'Unable to reach an agreement, ministers close debate on stem cells', *Europe Agri*, 5 December 2003.
[12] 'European parties clash on stem cells' 2006.

support of an increased budget for FP7.[13] Professor Austin Smith, director of the Welcome Trust Centre for Stem Cell Research in Cambridge, said that 'the problem here is one of a lack of scientific literacy and understanding that renders the public susceptible to an "odd alliance", which includes Greenpeace and the Vatican, both of which ignore the patient and the scientific evidence'.[14] The two coalitions defended fundamentally irreconcilable positions and EU policymakers were concerned that their pro-science agenda was going to be hampered.

Production and Mobilisation of Ethical Expertise

FP6 Negotiations

Deadlock over hESC Funding

As the agenda-setting debate for FP6 got under way, the issue of hESC research and its funding under the programme took centre stage. In its proposals for FP6, the European Commission placed genomics and biotechnology for health at the core of its strategy for strengthening European research and competitiveness.[15] The Commission's agenda provoked immediate reactions within the European Parliament and in some segments of the civil society. In August 2000, the UK Department of Health had already published a report recommending that research on human embryos for therapeutic purposes should be permitted,[16] in response to which the European Parliament had passed a resolution expressing its opposition to both reproductive and therapeutic cloning.[17] On the issue of hESC research, however, there was no consensus amongst MEPs. German, Italian and Austrian parliamentarians as well as most Green MEPs aimed to restrict the range of stem cell projects receiving EU funding, but a majority of MEPs were favourable to such research activities.[18] Within the Council of Ministers, member states defended highly diverse positions, framed in moral terms and presented as non-negotiable. Germany, Austria, Portugal and Italy threatened to block the adoption of the entire programme.[19]

---

[13] CORDIS 2005. [14] Nerlich 2012. [15] European Commission 2001a.
[16] Department of Health 2000. [17] European Parliament 2000.
[18] 'EU politicians say funding plan focuses too much on biotech, genomics' 2001.
[19] Ahlstrom 2003.

Technicalising the Debate and Delineating a Workable Policy Scenario

It is in this politically charged context that the President of the European Commission formally requested the advice of the EGE. DG RESEARCH, which is responsible for EU policies on the funding of research, was the DG the most interested in mobilising ethics experts. It expected, indeed, that their involvement in policy would facilitate the taming of the conflict that had surfaced over the funding of embryo research. In the words of an EU official, there was broad agreement within the European Commission that the EGE should be consulted 'because we had extreme positions at play' and 'in order to have a political agreement the EGE was of some help'.[20] EU officials expected ethics experts to be able to delineate a workable solution, and the experts also internalised that this was their task.

In Opinion 15, 'Ethical Aspects of Human Stem Cell Research',[21] ethics experts indeed succeeded in delineating an acceptable policy scenario. They did so by shifting the debate away from irreconcilable positions – either in support of or against hESC research – towards the *technicalities* of the issue. They differentiated amongst different 'types' of embryos and suggested that while spare (supernumerary) embryos are an appropriate source for stem cell research, the creation of embryos specifically for the purpose of stem cell procurement is ethically unacceptable 'since it represents a further step in the instrumentalisation of human life'.[22] To come to this conclusion, the EGE argued that the ethical acceptability of stem cell research depends not only on the objectives of the research but also on the source of the stem cells.[23] Essentially, the group justified this differentiation in very rational terms, by referring itself to the principle of proportionality, central to the doctrine of principlism. Concerning 'spare embryos', the EGE experts made it clear that given the potential of stem cell research to alleviate severe human sufferings, and the fact that in any case the embryos used for research need to be destroyed, there is no argument for excluding such research activities from funding.[24] Concerning the creation of embryos for the purpose of research, it argued instead that given the 'speculative hopes of regenerative medicine and the

---

[20] Interview with an official from DG Research, Ethics and Gender Division, 30 January 2013.
[21] European Group on Ethics 2000.
[22] European Group on Ethics 2000, p. 16.
[23] European Group on Ethics 2000, p. 13.
[24] European Group on Ethics 2000, p. 16.

availability of alternative sources of human stem cells', the use of such embryos would be premature.[25] The EGE experts explicitly invoked the need to respect proportionality between the objectives of research and the means used, explaining that 'remote therapeutic perspectives must be balanced against other considerations related to the risks of trivialising the use of the embryos'.[26] By reframing the debate in rational and technical terms, the EGE created the possibility of delineating a workable policy scenario.

Producing Ethical Expertise

The dynamics of the knowledge production process ensured that ethics experts would not diverge from the EU's agenda. Iterations between experts and EU policymakers manifested themselves in various forms throughout the production of the experts' opinion. At the time when the EGE started working on the issue of embryo research, its secretariat had been integrated into the Bureau of European Policy Advisors (BEPA) – the bureau that provides the European Commission policy advice and reports directly to the President of the Commission.[27] The integration of the EGE secretariat within the bureaucratic structure of the European Commission arguably ensured the Commission some degree of control over the EGE's work. In the words of an EGE expert, 'it was an attempt to tame the group [...] we were not consulted on that'.[28] If direct control is hard to evidence, the relocation of the EGE's secretariat definitely facilitated iterations between experts and policymakers, and associated phenomena of orchestration, ideational alignment and calibration throughout the process of knowledge production. According to an expert from the EGE, 'there is always a dialogue between the EGE and BEPA, the think tank of the president, when a request for an opinion is formulated'.[29]

Iterations also occurred in crossing points, those spaces where actors from different spheres – experts, policymakers and industry – work together. While the EGE was preparing its opinion, it organised

---

[25] European Group on Ethics 2000, p. 17.
[26] European Group on Ethics 2000, p. 17.
[27] BEPA was rebranded in 2014 as the European Political Strategy Centre (EPSC). At the same time the European Group of Ethics had been placed under the direct responsibility of Commissioner Carlos Moedas, the EU's Commissioner for Research, Science and Innovation.
[28] Interview with an expert from the EGE, 10 June 2013.
[29] Interview with an expert from the EGE, 13 April 2015.

a roundtable which gathered scientists, Commission officials and actors from the private sector. Representatives of the industry (Novartis; PPL Therapeutics) and of patients' organisations (European Parkinsonians) were convened. Commission officials – essentially from DG RESEARCH, but also from DG SANCO and the Directorate General for Enterprise and Industry (DG ENTR) – participated. Those who were invited to give a presentation during the roundtable were all scientists or representatives of patient organisations, and favoured hESC research.[30] Policy formulation was conducted within a closed policy community; with the exception of patient organisations, no other representatives of civil society participated.

Further instances of iterations took place through the circulation of individuals between institutions and the spanning of roles. For instance Goran Hermeren, appointed chair of the EGE in 2002, had also taken part in a research project on 'The Ethics of Human Stem Cell Research and Therapy in Europe' funded by the European Commission under the Fifth Framework Programme (FP5).[31] Thus, although the integration of BEPA within the structure of the Commission made it easy for EU policymakers to *orchestrate* the EGE's work, not much direct control was needed because a phenomenon of *ideational alignment* was also taking place. In the various crossing points described, policymakers and experts worked together, developed common ways of thinking on embryo research and formulated a common policy position – common to experts and policymakers alike.

On some occasions, ethics experts resisted the dominant policy discourse. This was the case for those experts who, often for ethical religious motives, had a more principled form of opposition towards embryo research.[32] Those experts nevertheless agreed to *calibrate* their position in order to meet the needs of the policy process. The EGE experts operated within a negotiating culture of conflict 'down toning', characteristic of the functioning of expert groups.[33] They also understood that their opinion had to be tied to existing possibilities for action and thus present a scenario acceptable to all actors in place. Once the EGE had delineated a solution, the European Commission was able to

---

[30] See the agenda at https://ec.europa.eu/archives/european_group_ethics/docs/agenda20_11_en.pdf.
[31] European Commission Research Directorate General 2001.
[32] Interviews with experts from the European Group on Ethics, April 2015.
[33] Robert 2010a, p. 27.

mobilise the opinion of the ethics experts as a legitimate end point in political negotiations. The EGE's recommendations on embryo research echoed the Commission's position, but benefited from a different, more epistemic, kind of authority.

Conflict Bypassing
Within the Council, member states easily reached consensus on some categories of research to be ruled out from EU funding, including research into reproductive human cloning, research into altering the genetic make-up of humans where alterations might be hereditary, and research involving the creation of human embryos solely for the purpose of securing stem cells.[34] They were, however, not able to find a consensus on hESC research conducted on supernumerary embryos. Italy under the Berlusconi government strongly objected to any funding for this type of research.[35] EU states eventually approved FP6 in the absence of agreement on the issue of hESC research. Although FP6 states that research involving the use of hESC can benefit from EU funding, member states decided that funding would in practice be suspended until they agreed on more specific provisions concerning such research activities.[36] The Commission and member states resolved to take a decision on the matter before December 2003 and that a moratorium would apply in the meantime.[37]

During this time, the European Commission continued to involve ethics experts in policymaking. In September 2001, DG RESEARCH organised a conference on 'Stem Cell Research at European Level', in order to 'consider the strategy for stem cell research at European level'.[38] The event gathered twelve out of the fifteen coordinators of scientific projects on stem cell research which were then funded by the Commission, Commission officials from DG RESEARCH and two experts from the EGE – Linda Nielsen, then vice-president of the EGE, and Octovi Quintana Trias, an EGE expert.[39] In December of the same year, Commissioner for Research Philippe Busquin initiated

---

[34] European Parliament and Council 2002.
[35] 'Renewed controversy on stem-cell research' 2002.
[36] European Parliament and Council 2002.
[37] 'Research: Council adopts specific programmes for FP6' 2002.
[38] European Commission Research Directorate General 2001, p. 2.
[39] European Commission Research Directorate General 2001; see list of participants at the event, pp. 19–21.

another conference on 'Stem Cells: Therapies for the Future?' which gathered ethics experts from the EGE, industry representatives, commission officials and scientists.[40] These crossing points allowed policymakers and experts – traditional scientific experts as well as ethics experts – to work together on a regular basis. The convening of a narrowly delineated set of actors, who reflected on policy behind closed doors, also contributed to contain conflict within a closed policy community.

In April 2003, the European Commission issued a report on human embryonic stem cell research, which formulated its policy proposals on the issue.[41] The report repeatedly cites the opinion of the EGE in order to give epistemic authority to the proposals. In the wake of the report, the Commission organised an inter-institutional seminar on bioethics, composed of scientific, legal and ethics experts, as well as representatives of the European Parliament, the Council and member states. By involving ethics experts again in the policy process, EU policymakers made their proposals and the agreement reached during the meeting hard to dispute. 'On the basis of the outcome of the meeting', the Commission proposed draft guidelines on the applications of FP6, which essentially backed hESC research, arguing that embryo research promises to alleviate the 'suffering of so many patients who currently have no hope of an adequate cure'.[42] It claimed that its policy proposals were 'based on the principles established by the European Group on Ethics, especially the fundamental ethical principles underlined in the opinion No. 15'.[43]

A year later, however, member states had still not been able to reach consensus on the application provisions of hESC research. In December 2003, the Italian presidency tabled a compromise, which contained important restrictions to embryo research; in particular it put forward that such research should only use stem cell lines created before December 2003.[44] States that had restrictive domestic regimes on hESC research, such as Spain, Portugal, Germany, Luxembourg and Austria, backed the proposal. DG RESEARCH, for its part, opposed the text; Philippe Busquin insisted that introducing

---

[40] European Commission 2001b. [41] European Commission 2003a.
[42] European Commission 2003a, p. 2. [43] European Commission 2003a, p. 5.
[44] 'EU votes on stem cells fail to solve problem' 2003.

a deadline for stem cell lines would significantly restrict the scope for research, thus technicalising the debate.[45] Within the Council, the proposed text failed to secure the qualified majority required.[46] Strikingly, EU policymakers then used the stalemate within the Council in order to recapture full control over policy. The Commission decided that it would apply the FP6 as adopted by the Council in September 2002, thus de facto authorising the funding of hESC research. Philippe Busquin announced that since the moratorium on European Community research using stem cells was about to expire, 'the European Commission is henceforth responsible for the management of the framework programme'.[47] In order to justify its decision to fund research conducted on supernumerary embryos, the European Commission once again reasserted that its proposal was fully in line with the opinion of the EGE.[48] By resorting to the use of ethics experts, the Commission was able to recapture control over policy despite the politicisation of the debate.

Involving the EGE in the process permitted, first, the reintroduction of a *degree of technicality* into ongoing discussions. Formerly entrenched policy positions were reframed in a series of more technical policy solutions, and this in turn made the delineating of a *complex policy scenario* possible. The solution proposed by the EGE then acted as a *legitimate end point* in policy debates, which ultimately allowed the Commission to apply the FP6 programme despite the blatant politicisation of the debate and an absence of agreement amongst states. Involving ethics experts did more than tame conflict; it acted as a tool to *bypass* it. Their mobilisation could play such functions in the policy process because the position of the EGE echoed that of EU policymakers. Knowledge orchestration by policymakers, ideational alignment through repeated iterations between experts and policymakers, and efforts from experts themselves to calibrate their claims in order to meet the needs of the policy debate resulted in the shaping of an 'acceptable' policy position – shared by experts and policymakers alike and which could hardly be contested beyond this circle.

[45] 'Unable to reach an agreement, ministers close debate on stem cells' 2003.
[46] Council of the European Union 2003.
[47] Cited in 'Unable to reach an agreement' 2003.
[48] European Commission 2003b.

FP7 Negotiations

Renewed Controversy over the Funding of Embryo Research

During the negotiations on FP7, debates over the funding of hESCs reopened along very similar lines. Member states opposed to hESC research bolstered their discourse by arguing that their contributions to the EU budget should not be used to fund research permitted only in 'liberal' EU countries. The 'liberal' coalition, on its side, reiterated that embryo research held great potential for the treatment of certain diseases such as Parkinson's, Alzheimer's or spinal cord injuries and promised to boost the EU's competitiveness.

The 'conservative' coalition became increasingly active in 2005, following a highly mediatised scandal concerning some eggs that had, allegedly, been illegally traded to the UK.[49] In this context, the European Parliament adopted a resolution in March 2005 calling for the principle of subsidiarity to be applied to the funding of hESC research.[50] The resolution received considerable support with over 300 MEPs voting in favour and only 200 against.[51] It is in this context that the European Commission issued its proposals in September 2005, suggesting, essentially, that the FP6 compromise concerning hESC funding be maintained.[52] Unsurprisingly, the Commission's proposals provoked immediate reaction within the European Parliament. A group of seventy-three MEPs signed a letter addressed to Commission President Barroso, asking him to exercise his influence to ensure that funding for embryo research would not take place under FP7.[53] The overwhelming majority of signatories were from Eastern European member states and members of the EPP-ED group.[54]

A year later, however, the anti-hESC research coalition was not able to gather sufficient support in the European Parliament and a majority of MEPs voted in favour of hESC funding when examining the Commission's proposals on FP7. From then on, the debate moved to the Council of Ministers, where a group of member states threatened to veto the adoption of FP7. Under the leadership of Annette Schavan, then German minister of education and research, a letter was sent to the Finnish presidency of the Council in July 2006 stating, in particular, that 'the European Union science programme should not be used to

---

[49] Rudebeck 2005.   [50] European Parliament 2005.   [51] Plomer 2008, p. 848.
[52] European Commission 2005a.
[53] 'MEPs sound alarm on stem cell research' 2005.   [54] Plomer 2008.

give financial incentives to kill embryos'.[55] With the entry of Eastern European states into the EU, it became clear that a group of member states might be able to prevent an agreement within the Council.

Orchestration

In an attempt to tame this divisive debate, the European Commission adopted a proactive role and drafted a declaration – later labelled the 'hESC compromise declaration' – concerning the conditions for hESC research to be eligible for funding. In November of the same year, the president of the European Commission requested the EGE to provide an opinion 'on the implementing measures required during the ethics review of research projects on hESCs [under FP7] that will assure that the ethical rules and requirements are fully met'.[56] He asked the group to *not* deliberate again on the ethics of hESC research, but only on its *modalities*. In a speech which he gave to the EGE experts in February 2007, Janez Potočnik, then commissioner for research, explained that:

> For the 7th Framework Programme, the agreement found between the three institutions, the Commission, the European Parliament and the Council, is to continue the ethical framework of the FP6 and the specific procedure set up for human embryonic stem cell research. I can assure you that the compromise found for Community funding of human embryonic stem cell research is not only the best possible agreement on this issue but probably the only possible one.[57]

In narrowing down the question it asked the EGE on the modalities of hESC research, the Commission ensured that the very principle of hESC research funding would not be reopened to debate. This was seen as crucial by the Commission services because the EGE was, since 2005, perceived as dominated by 'conservative' views.[58] Since its 2005 reshuffling, the EGE included experts whose religious affiliation was publicly known.[59] The perceived change in the orientation of the group was criticised by scientists, who argued that the new nominations were based on 'political and religious considerations'.[60] Changes in the composition of the group naturally affected the way in which the

---

[55] Cited in 'Germany calls for EU ban on stem cell research' 2006.
[56] European Group on Ethics 2007a, p. 21.   [57] Potočnik 2007.
[58] Interviews in Brussels, October 2012.
[59] Interviews with EU officials, October 2012.   [60] Bosch 2005.

European Commission could mobilise its expertise. EU policymakers were thus careful to reopen the debate on embryo research and only ask the group about the modalities of the ethics review process.

Also, because the Commission was well aware that several members of the EGE were not favourable to embryo research, EU officials made sure that they presented their views to the experts. Several officials from DG RESEARCH discussed with them before the group issued its opinion. Octavi Quintana Trias, director of the Health Unit of DG RESEARCH, gave a talk to the EGE in January 2007.[61] In his presentation he reiterated all the existing and potential benefits of hESC research, in particular concerning regenerative medicine, in an attempt to frame embryo research as scientifically promising. At the same time, Jean-Michel Baer, another official from DG RESEARCH, gave the group a presentation on 'Integrating Ethics in EU Research'. In his talk he discussed the ethical review process for research funded under FP7, reassuring the EGE experts that the ethical review process would ensure that proposals 'are in line with the Opinion 15 of the EGE' and that 'independent experts assess the necessity of using hESC for achieving the objectives set forth in the proposal'.[62]

In June 2007, the EGE eventually issued its *Recommendations on the Ethical Review of hESC FP7 Research Projects*.[63] It used its mandate extensively and set strict requirements concerning the modalities of hESC research. The EGE experts proposed, first, that 'if alternatives to hESCs with the same scientific potential as embryo-derived stem cells will be found in the future, their use should be maximized'.[64] Moreover, the EGE stated that in addition to the ethical review, hESC-related project proposals should undergo a scientific review, which should address issues such as whether the research objectives could be achieved with alternatives to hESC and whether the applicants could demonstrate that their research was aimed at improving human health or boosting biomedical knowledge. The concept of human dignity took a central place in the reasoning of the EGE. It was creatively mobilised, in particular, in order to also justify that animals, rather than hECSs, be used for toxicity testing of industrial chemicals such as drugs or

---

[61] See http://ec.europa.eu/archives/european_group_ethics/archive/2005_2010/activities/docs/quintana_trias_en.pdf.
[62] Presentation from Michel Bauer: http://ec.europa.eu/archives/european_group_ethics/archive/2005_2010/activities/docs/jm_baer_en.pdf.
[63] European Group on Ethics 2007a.   [64] European Group on Ethics 2007a.

cosmetics.[65] But fundamentally – and despite its changed composition – the EGE did not go beyond the position that remained acceptable to the European Commission, thus calibrating its claims to that effect. Its opinion essentially reiterated the position of the European Commission, with the exception of its recommendations on animal testing.

Conflict Manoeuvring
Involving ethics experts in policy facilitated the adoption of FP7. It acted as a means of reassuring the 'conservative' coalition that strict requirements would apply at the reviewing stage of projects submitted for funding, while at the same time facilitating the Commission's policy concerning hESC research. The mobilisation of ethical expertise played a role in acting as a form of 'ethics warrant' for states that were most sceptical towards embryo research. Before the EGE issued its opinion, Janez Potočnik, then research commissioner, stated that the opinion would ensure that FP7 would be 'acceptable to the majority of the scientists, but also importantly to the majority of the member states'.[66] Member states indeed reached a political agreement at an extraordinary meeting of the Council in July 2006, thus enabling the European Parliament to move ahead with its second reading.[67] The compromise adopted by member states contained the commitment to not fund any activities that 'destroy human embryos', but accepted the funding of research on 'subsequent steps involving human embryonic stem cells',[68] essentially replicating the FP6 compromise. Lithuania, Austria, Malta, Slovakia and Poland voted against the agreement, but Germany, Italy and Luxembourg switched from the 'no' camp to back the compromise. The assurance that the EGE would itself pronounce on the modalities of hESC research was central to securing support from opposing member states within the Council. In fact, no agreement would have been reached without the guarantee that the EGE would issue an opinion on the implementation of FP7.[69] The European Parliament and member states eventually approved FP7 at the end of 2006.

[65] European Group on Ethics 2007a. [66] Potočnik 2007.
[67] 'Competitive council: Political deal secured on 7th framework research programme' 2006.
[68] Council of the European Union 2006, p. 7.
[69] Interview with members of the EGE, 2 September 2012.

At a time when the composition of the EGE had changed, EU policymakers carefully orchestrated the EGE's work. By asking the EGE to focus strictly on the modalities of the ethics review process, the Commission ensured that the *principle* of embryo research funding would not be re-examined. By presenting their views to the experts, policymakers also clearly delineated what solutions were considered 'acceptable'. At the same time, involving ethics experts in policy provided an 'ethics warrant' to more conservative states, by reassuring them that strict standards would be set on the modalities of hESC research, thus making the compromise acceptable to them. Here, involving ethics experts in policy tamed policy conflict, but it did so in a very special way: the opinion produced by the experts allowed policymakers to manoeuvre through the conflict by giving the appearance that the EGE acted as a counterweight to the Commission's pro-research position. In reality, the EGE opinion, because of the dynamics that characterised the process of knowledge production, did not contain any critique of the Commission's position.

Conclusions

European Commission bureaucrats mobilised ethics experts as a means to bypass or tame the highly polarised policy conflict which had surfaced over the funding of hESC research. The European Commission was able to mobilise the experts' opinions and make the funding of hESC research possible *despite the lack of agreement amongst member states and the social actors involved*. Ethics expertise acted as a crucial mechanism to bypass or manoeuvre through political conflict.

Experts could not have performed such a role in policy if their opinions had not been produced iteratively between the expert and the policy spheres. EU policymakers were able to *orchestrate* the EGE's work in various ways, and thus ensure that ethics experts could not diverge from its own agenda. They presented their views to the EGE experts, made them well aware of the possible contours of political action and strictly delineated the remit of their reflection in the case of FP7. But such orchestration was often effortless, because policymakers and experts had already worked together in various crossing points and developed common ways of thinking on embryo research.

Even after the reshuffling of the EGE in 2005 and EU policymakers' anxiety that the ethics group would diverge from its own agenda, alternative expert voices were not capable of destabilising the EU's pro-science discourse. Orchestration, ideational alignment and calibration acted as efficient mechanisms of stabilisation, countering divergent voices within the expert sphere, and thus allowing the mobilisation of bioethics to act as an efficient way of manoeuvring though conflicts concerning scientific and technological controversies.

5 | *Manipulating Particles on a Small Scale*

Checking the Rise of Conflict

This chapter examines the production and mobilisation of ethics expertise in the case of EU nanotechnology policy. Since the mid-1990s, in an attempt to compete with US initiatives in the field, the European Commission has attempted to push the development of research on nanotechnologies. As conventionally understood, the term 'nanotechnology' refers to the design or manipulation of structures and devices at a scale of 1 to 100 nanometres (or hundred thousandths of a metre). The ability to manipulate particles on an atomic and molecular scale already has a broad range of applications in domains as diverse as cosmetics, food packaging, water-resistant textiles and drugs, to name a few. In the early 2000s, US and EU policymakers alike framed nanotechnologies as a potentially revolutionary source of progress in health and wealth more broadly. But environmental NGOs and Green parties in Europe voiced their concerns about the potential environmental and health risks of nanotechnologies, mentioning in particular the capability of nanoparticles to penetrate the blood–brain barrier and the risks of exposure to nanomaterials that have dispersed in air, aquatic environments, soil and sediments. It is in this context that the European Commission decided to involve ethics experts in policy. Former Commission president Manuel Barroso sent a formal request to the EGE in March 2005, asking its experts to examine the ethical implications of nanomedicine.

The chapter brings to light that the mobilisation of ethics experts checked the rise of a potential conflict in the development of nanotechnology research and its associated industrial applications. For the European Commission, it was crucial that the 'push for nanos' would not be hampered by citizens' protests. The protests which had crystallised around GMOs, understood by the Commission services as a downright communication failure between its officials and the public, loomed large. EU policymakers wanted to avoid a 'GM repeat' at all costs. Involving ethics experts in policy made it possible for EU officials to pre-empt an expansion to the broader public of the policy conflict on nanotechnologies. By showcasing that a new type of experts representing a diversity of voices had been consulted, the European Commission in fact ensured that policy remained formulated within a closed community composed of EU officials, experts and the industry. By consulting ethics experts the European Commission also endowed its proposals with epistemic authority, thus shielding itself from potential critique. These concerns were particularly crucial in the field of nanomedicine, which raised anxieties in the broader public. But at the same time, by asking the EGE to focus solely on ethical issues of nanomedicine, EU policymakers successfully framed other environmental and health safety issues related to nanotechnologies as *technical* issues, better dealt with through an improvement of existing tests and procedures than with legislative reforms. Essentially, both the European Commission and the EGE argued that safety and toxicology concerns were not ethical concerns, thus allowing for a compartmentalisation of ethics and a technicalisation of the debate.

The mobilisation of ethics experts successfully contained conflict because ethics expertise was produced in an iterative space between experts and policymakers. The European Commission informed the EGE about the tenets of the policy debate as well as its policy preferences. It also gave substantial information to the EGE experts, who were not all familiar with the specificities of nanotechnologies and their implications. But orchestration was facilitated by the ideational alignment that occurred between experts and those who were shaping policy within the European Commission. EU policymakers and ethics experts worked together in various crossing points, such as BEPA, conferences, workshops and roundtables, where a common way of looking at the policy problem progressively developed. Orchestration and ideational alignment effectively stabilised the bioethical discourse on nanotechnologies, so that bioethics could in turn be mobilised to pre-empt an expansion of the conflict to the civil society at large.

The Policy Controversy over 'Nanos'

The Push for Nanos

Since the mid-1990s, DG RESEARCH within the European Commission has sought to promote nanotechnology research, technical development, and demonstration (RTD). Nanotechnology RTD was already a major priority under the Fifth Framework Programme (1998–2002), which significantly expanded the scope of nanoscientific research and development. But the turning point in EU nanotechnology policy took place in reaction to US initiatives in the field. In 2000, Bill Clinton launched the National Nanotechnology Initiative (NNI), which planned to significantly invest in nanotechnologies. The NNI triggered an extraordinary amount of hype; the White House itself talked of the NNI as 'leading to the next industrial revolution'.[1] US investments were perceived as a threat to industrial counterparts in Europe, and in a typical instance of innovation race, directly triggered EU efforts to also invest in the sector.[2] Philippe Busquin, then Commissioner for Research within the European Commission, clearly explained that given that 'the US government is pouring 600 to 700 million dollars per year into this sector', the Commission 'will respond by allocating more than EUR 700 million to nanotechnology research over four years within the forthcoming 6th Research Framework Programme (2003–2006)'.[3] Renzo Tomellini, then head of the Nano and Converging Sciences and Technologies Unit within DG RESEARCH (the 'Nanotechnology Unit'), sums up that 'we wanted to be the best, we wanted to be number one'.[4] In its 2005 'Nanosciences and Nanotechnologies: An Action Plan for Europe 2005–2009', the European Commission proposed to further boost research in nanotechnologies in the EU with the launch of the Seventh Framework Programme.[5]

In this context, DG RESEARCH, supported by DG for Health and Consumers (DG SANCO), which strongly believed in the potential of nanomedicine, and DG for Enterprise and Industry (DG ENTR), started developing a discourse which claimed, all at the same time, that nanotechnologies will eradicate poverty, hunger and drudgery. In a typical instance of pro-science and innovation bias, the European Commission framed nanotechnologies as a 'new industrial revolution' which would include breakthroughs in sectors as diverse as computer

[1] White House 2000.
[2] Interview with an official from DG RESEARCH, 3 December 2014.
[3] Fabio Fabbi, 'Commission to invest Euro 700 million in nanotechnology research', *Times Higher Education*, 13 June 2002.
[4] Interview with Renzo Tomellini, *Euractiv*, 17 November 2003, at: www.euractiv.com/section/nanotechnology/news/is-nanotechnology-dangerous-we-need-to-know-says-renzo-tomellini.
[5] European Commission 2005b.

efficiency, pharmaceuticals, nerve and tissue repair, surface coatings, catalysts, sensors, materials, telecommunications and pollution control.[6] In order to promote a smooth and fast development of the EU's nanotechnology strategy, the 'pro-nano' DGs wanted to avoid strict regulation of the field and favoured the regulation of nanomaterials under existing regulatory structures. In its 2004 communication, the European Commission stated that 'maximum use should be made of existing regulation'.[7] DG SANCO also identified the use of existing legislative structures as 'the only realistic option'.[8] For EU policymakers, 'nano-related' research had to be promoted quickly, smoothly and under the existing regulatory framework.

Protests from the Greens

The European Commission's plans immediately triggered protests from Green parties, NGOs and a handful of high-profile individuals who contributed to publicise the issue. Prince Charles (a long time 'green activist' and already a vocal critic of GMOs) played a key role in attracting public attention to the risks of nanotechnologies in the UK. In June 2003, he triggered media attention by calling upon the UK Royal Society – which serves as the UK's national scientific academy – to evaluate the risks of nanotechnology.[9] The Royal Society, together with the Royal Academy of Engineers, agreed to conduct a study to define what is meant by nanotechnology, assess the potential health, safety and environmental impacts of such technologies, consider ethical and social issues, and identify areas where additional regulation needs to be considered. The study marked a watershed in the debate by acknowledging the potential adverse consequences of nanotechnologies – in

---

[6] European Commission 2004a.   [7] European Commission 2004a, p. 18.
[8] The Risk Assessment Unit of DG SANCO identified five possible regulatory approaches and weighed them against one another: (1) adopting a 'laissez-faire' attitude; (2) decreeing a moratorium on nanotechnologies research and development (R&D) and/or commercialisation; (3) relying on voluntary measures; (4) launching a comprehensive, in-depth regulatory process specific to nanotechnologies; (5) launching an incremental process using existing legislative structures. Option 1 was considered 'unwise'; option 2 was deemed impossible 'because nanotechnologies have already entered the market and their ubiquitous and horizontal nature makes them difficult to control'; option 3 had 'little appeal because voluntary measures generally prove ineffective'; option 4 was 'difficult because of the scope'; leaving option 5 as 'the only realistic option' (European Commission 2004b).
[9] Highfield 2003.

particular when nanomaterials 'cross the blood–brain barrier and other natural defence mechanisms of the human body'.[10] The report concludes, essentially, that nanoparticles are potentially hazardous and therefore must be regulated as new substances.

At the same time, concerns over the risks of nanotechnologies were voiced by the Green Party within the European Parliament, as well as a group of active NGOs. In June 2003, the Greens, Greenpeace, the Dag Hammarskjold Foundation, Genewatch UK and Clean Production Action held the first international seminar on the societal impacts of nanotechnology at the European Parliament. Several scientists were also invited to present their views. Doug Parr, chief scientist with Greenpeace in the UK, smartly evoked the debate over GMOs in order to remind policymakers that 'policy must not be composed by small groups of experts and bureaucrats'.[11] It was also on this occasion that Caroline Lucas (UK MEP and leader of the UK Green Party) invited a Canadian NGO, the Action Group on Erosion, Technology and Concentration (ETC Group), to present their position on nanotechnologies. The ETC Group holds a strict precautionary stance on nanotechnologies, already publicised in *The Big Down* in January 2003.[12] The ETC Group acted as a leader in the anti-nano campaign, and propagated sensationalist depictions of nanotechnologies. It warned, for instance, that 'mass production of unique nanomaterials and self-replicating nano-machinery pose incalculable risks' and that 'atomtech [nanotechnology] could also mean the creation and combination of new elements and the amplification of weapons of mass destruction'.[13] The main thrust of the contributions at the seminar was, thus, clearly hostile to the European Commission's nanotechnology programme. Caroline Lucas called on the Commission to mainstream safety concerns.[14] Pointing to the lack of available knowledge on the impacts of nanotechnology, she called for a moratorium on certain aspects of nanotechnology use and research until a strict regulatory framework could be put in place, 'including regulations on liability for the negative impacts of nanotech and strict labelling requirements and compulsory assessments of their effects'.[15] For the Greens, as well as the NGOs involved, nanoparticles were to be classified as new

---

[10] Royal Society and Royal Academy of Engineers 2004, p. 41.
[11] Royal Society and Royal Academy of Engineers 2004, p. 41.
[12] Action Group on Erosion, Technology and Concentration (ETC Group) 2003.
[13] Action Group on Erosion, Technology and Concentration (ETC Group) 2003.
[14] CORDIS 2003.   [15] Lucas 2003.

substances, and *nano-specific regulations* should be set in place. Progressively, a fault line emerged between stakeholders with an interest in managing nanomaterials under the existing regulatory architecture of the EU, and a more cautious group asking for new regulation.

In 2005 the European Commission published *Nanosciences and Nanotechnologies: An Action Plan for Europe 2005–2009*, which proposed to boost research in nanotechnologies in the EU with the launch of the Seventh Framework Programme.[16] The Action Plan was strongly influenced by the industry, which by then directly participated to the formulation of the EU nanotechnology agenda through the European Technology Platform (ETP) for Nanomedicine. Set up in 2005, the ETP for Nanomedicine gathers together – in a typical instance of closed policy community – the nanotech industry, research institutions and EU policymakers. Its self-proclaimed objective consists in producing strategic documents for EU nanotechnology.[17] The Commission's Action Plan provoked further protests from the Greens in the European Parliament. MEP Hiltrud Breyer (Greens) explained during a parliamentary debate:

We have just heard that nano-particles are capable of crossing the blood/brain barrier. Knowing as we do of these risks, surely we have to put protective mechanisms in place? We cannot simply allow these products to be put onto the market and tested on consumers; we cannot allow consumers to be treated as guinea pigs! … I see it as positively irresponsible that the Commission, even though it knows what is missing and is aware of the lack of any methodology for assessing the risks, wants to allow the marketing of consumer goods aimed at private citizens and their households, without the certainty of every risk having been removed.[18]

These concerns were immediately echoed by Green NGOs. In May 2006, Friends of the Earth issued a report focusing on the risks of nanomaterials in sunscreens and cosmetics, proposing to place a moratorium on the commercialisation of nanoproducts until safety research could be conducted.[19] Like Greenpeace, Friends of the Earth expressed its concern that existing legislation was not adequate.

[16] European Commission 2005b.
[17] Website of ETP for Nanomedicine, https://etp-nanomedicine.eu.
[18] See the debate in the European Parliament: www.europarl.europa.eu/sides/getDoc.do?type=CRE&reference=20060928&secondRef=ITEM-004&language=EN&ring=A6-2006-0216.
[19] Miller et al. 2006.

Consumer organisations also criticised the European Commission for not addressing the regulatory deficits identified by scientists and civil society organisations.[20]

DG SANCO, DG RESEARCH and DG ENTR continued on their side to reject the need for nano-specific regulations. Instead, they promoted an approach focused on better implementing existing legislation and developing methods for evaluating risks through technical tools. An official from DG RESEARCH explains that 'the regulatory framework does not need to be modified, but the evaluation of risks needs to be'.[21] The Scientific Committee on Emerging and Newly Identified Health Risks (SCENIHR), housed at DG SANCO, began investigating the appropriateness of existing methodologies to assess the potential risks associated with nanotechnologies. The committee concluded in its report that 'conventional toxicity and ecotoxicity tests have already been shown to be useful in evaluating the hazards of nanoparticles. However, some methods may require modification and some new testing methods may also be needed'.[22] In 2008 the European Commission led by DG ENTR issued a communication on the regulatory aspects of nanomaterials, which reaffirmed that current community legislation generally covered nanomaterials risks, and that no changes are necessary apart from improving testing methods.[23] By then, this position was easier to sustain given the entry into force of the REACH (Registration, Evaluation, Authorisation and Restriction of Chemical Substances) regulation.[24] REACH was a major success for Green parties, national environmental ministers throughout Europe and 'Green' NGOs. It was adopted despite heavy resistance on the part of the industry and some EU states. One of the most important components of the REACH regulation was a major shift in the burden of risk assessment from public authorities to manufacturers. This reallocation of accountability is important for the nanotechnology debate because it at the same time satisfies the Green lobby, while effectively absolving the Commission of the responsibility to conduct such

---

[20] European Consumer Voice in Standardisation (ANEC) and European Consumers' Organisation (BEUC) 2009.
[21] Interview with an official from DG SANCO, 19 March 2015.
[22] Scientific Committee on Emerging and Newly Identified Health Risks (SCENIHR) 2007, pp. 59–60.
[23] European Commission 2008a, pp. 3, 8.
[24] European Parliament and Council 2006.

assessments. Although REACH had very little to do with nanotechnology, EU officials framed REACH as the adequate framework for the regulation for nanomaterials. According to DG ENTR, nanomaterials are de facto regulated by REACH because they are covered by the definition of a chemical 'substance' included in REACH.[25] This view was not defended unanimously, even within the European Commission. Eva Hellsten, an official from DG ENTR, claimed that inclusion of nanomaterials in the REACH regulation is 'somewhat problematic, because although nanomaterials resemble chemicals, the novel nanomaterial properties being developed make them different'.[26] The position of the 'pro-nanos' DGs of the European Commission was threefold. First, the regulation of nanomaterials within the existing regulatory framework was adequate. Second, if any effort was needed, it consisted in targeting methods of risk evaluation. Third, high reliance on self-regulation was to be promoted.

On the one hand, the European Commission, together with the industry and a majority of scientists, wanted to push research and new applications in the field quickly and smoothly. On the other, they were concerned that the nano agenda would stir opposition from Green parties, consumers and European citizens. It was in this context that Commission President Manuel Barroso formally asked the experts of the EGE to produce an opinion on nanomedicine.

Production and Mobilisation of Ethical Expertise

EU policymakers mobilised ethics experts with a specific agenda in mind. The DGs that pushed for 'nanos' wanted to pre-empt opposition to the development of nanotechnologies through a double-edged

---

[25] See also European Chemicals Agency (ECHA) n.d. The position of the European Commission was similar in relation to nanodrugs. It argued, essentially, that medicinal products making use of nanomaterials can be dealt with under the current legislative framework – either under the general 2001 medicines directive or the relevant directives on medical devices. Unsurprisingly, the ETP for Nanomedicine also stated that 'it is important to underline that nanomedicine is not a new category of healthcare products, but rather a new enabling technology used in the design and production of medical devices and pharmaceuticals' and that 'for this reason general legislation on medicines and medical devices applies' (European Technology Platform for Nanomedicine 2005).

[26] EURACTIV 2007.

strategy of *policy insulation* – under the cloak of an integrated dialogue strategy – and *issue technicalisation*, in practice by circumscribing the relevance of 'ethics' to a narrow set of issues. In order to do this, EU policymakers had to make sure that ethics experts echoed their position. To that effect, they deployed a strategy of knowledge orchestration. But they did not need to do much. Because ethics experts had already worked together with EU officials throughout the drafting of their opinion, a process of ideational alignment had already occurred.

The Spectre of the GMO Precedent

The protests from Green MEPs and NGOs raised strong concerns within the European Commission; the EU's push for nanotechnology research took place against the background of the GMO precedent, and EU officials were wary of a similar scenario. When GM agro-food products, already commercialised in the United States, began to be exported to Europe in the mid-1990s, the European Commission had indeed not been able to pre-empt a wave of civil society protests. A group of NGOs, including Greenpeace and Friends of the Earth, initiated strong campaigns against US imports. High-profile personalities such as Prince Charles, as well as famous scientists, swiftly joined in the debate. Consumers also started boycotting GM agro-food products. Major supermarket chains began excluding GM ingredients from their own-brand food products, while the food industry started labelling to guarantee the absence of GM products in foodstuffs.[27] Several EU member states refused to accept the market consents of GM crops. This de facto moratorium blocked the commercialisation of GM agro-food products in the EU. A highly ranked official from DG RESEARCH clearly summarises his DG's thinking, explaining that 'GM food was a technological success, an industry success, and a complete market failure' but that 'this was not the fault of a single policy or practice, but instead the result of not taking a holistic approach to technology'.[28] EU policymakers essentially perceived the 'GMO story' as that of a communication failure between European citizens, on the one hand, and the elite and experts, on the other. An interviewed official from DG RESEARCH could not be clearer on this

---

[27] Devos et al. 2006.
[28] Interview with an official from DG RESEARCH, 4 December 2014.

when he explained that he was hired specifically 'to prevent another GM story'.[29]

Opening Up the Debate, but to Whom?

Thus, when the European Commission decided to boost nanotechnology investments, the shadow of the GMO case loomed large, and EU officials decided to proceed differently. EU policymakers laid out what they themselves labelled an *anticipatory and inclusive approach*. Renzo Tomellini, then head of DG RESEARCH's Nanotechnology Unit, played a central role in promoting this approach 'to establish a dialogue with all representatives of the civil society'.[30] EU policymakers made it clear that 'it is in the common interest to adopt a proactive stance and fully integrate societal considerations into the R&D process', and that 'this needs to be carried out as early as possible and not simply expecting acceptance post-facto'.[31]

An official from DG RESEARCH explains that:

Markets are about people and people may not be scientists ... but they are not stupid. We can't explain things in scientific terms, but we can develop science-based information and provide it publicly. This is not brainwashing, it is logical communication. We wanted to use everything at our disposal to get the message across about nanotechnology. We used social media and '*cercle citoyen*'. It was really a different approach, but the necessary approach to guarantee success.[32]

The industry, well aware of the potential risks of neglecting dialogue with the public, also claimed to be in favour of an anticipatory inclusion of social concerns in the policy process. The ETP for Nanomedicine, which worked in symbiosis with EU policymakers, explained in its 2005 'Vision Paper and Basis for a Strategic Research Agenda for NanoMedicine' that 'acceptance of NanoMedicine necessitates transparent and timely information of all stakeholders, including the general public'.[33] At the same time, when the ETP details how it envisions putting this goal into practice, it only recommends that 'new

---

[29] Interview with an official from DG SANCO, 19 March 2015.
[30] Interview with an official from DG SANCO, 19 March 2015.
[31] European Commission 2004a, p. 19.
[32] Interview with an official from DG RESEARCH, 4 December 2014.
[33] European Technology Platform for Nanomedicine 2005, p. 33.

nanomedical inventions have to be evaluated for new ethical aspects by ethical, legal and social aspects specialists'.[34] For both the European Commission and the industry, social concerns were to be included, essentially, via the expansion of the policy debate to *ethics experts, rather than the public*. Thus, in the same year the Nano2Life Network, an FP6 Network of Excellence established in 2004, founded the first European Ethical, Legal, and Social Aspects (ELSA) board in the field.[35] Most efforts on the part of EU policymakers consisted in setting up ethics boards and involving ethics specialists in policy formulation. And when the policy process was opened to other actors, it was mainly to nanotech companies and scientists, in effect keeping policy formulation controlled by a closed policy community.

Involving the EGE experts in the policy process was an essential component of the European Commission's integrated and anticipatory approach. EU policymakers decided to involve ethics experts at a very early stage of the policy process. The EGE started working on the issue of nanomedicine in 2004. At the time, nanomedicine was the object of considerable 'hype' – it appeared to be the aspect of nanotechnology policy that was going to move the fastest and have the greatest implications, in particular in relation to cancer drugs. Such a discourse typically characterises the cycle of a new technology, with 'some who claim that we have something all powerful, all good, and that we know exactly where this goes'.[36] But at the same time, nanomedicine was the domain that crystallised the greatest fears. Nanomedicine indeed confronts a cross section of ethical questions beyond the toxicological concerns shared by other industries. In the field of diagnostics, nanotechnology gathers data on patients that could be used for profit, prompting ethical questions about data protection. The ETP for Nanomedicine also stressed that 'nanotechnology will add a new dimension to the bio (human) and non-bio (machine) interface such as brain chips or implants, which eventually might raise new ethical issues specific to NanoMedicine' and that for this reason careful analysis of ethical aspects by ethics committees at the European scale' is required.[37] Because of all the hype but also the associated fears,

[34] European Technology Platform for Nanomedicine 2005, p. 34.
[35] See CORDIS 2012.
[36] Interview with an official from the International Center for Technology Assessment (ICTA), 10 June 2016.
[37] European Technology Platform for Nanomedicine 2005, p. 33.

developments in nanomedicine promised to be the most controversial aspect of the EU's agenda related to nanotechnologies. EU policymakers anticipated this and decided to address potential anxieties by involving ethics experts early on.

An official from DG RESEARCH explained that 'it was the first time that ethics experts were involved so early on' and that 'there had been a learning process' since other attempts to introduce technological innovations, as the EGE was involved even before any kind of opposition arose.[38] For EU officials, it was crucial to involve the EGE experts in order to ensure they could not be 'attacked' or 'criticised for being ignorant or not diligent.'[39] The early involvement of the EGE can, therefore, be understood as part of the European Commission's strategy to pre-empt opposition to its policies and facilitate a smooth ascent for nanotechnology in the EU.[40] As expressed by an advisor from BEPA, 'all civil society responses were anticipated and we jumped the gun to incorporate public concerns first – *not to counter them, but to pre-empt and incorporate them*'.[41] The moderate opposition that coalesced around Green MEPs and their NGO counterparts could be channelled into the anticipatory and inclusive framework developed by the European Commission.

Ethics specialists acted as a core apparatus of policymaking for EU policymakers. Their mobilisation allowed the European Commission to claim that ethical and social concerns had been incorporated without in fact opening up the formulation policy more broadly. A closer examination at the European Commission's engagement with stakeholders in the field reveals, indeed, that civil society associations did not have much weight in the agenda of EU policymakers. EU officials worked together with representatives of the industry as well as experts: networks of scientists who contributed with expertise through EU-funded projects, specifically appointed expert groups and the ethics experts from the EGE. In this context, Greenpeace clearly expressed its concern that the industry just wanted 'to launch pre-emptive strikes against any problems with public acceptance of nanotechnology that might arise down the line'.[42] The integrated and anticipatory approach

[38] Interview with an official from DG RESEARCH, 5 December 2014.
[39] Interview with an official from DG RESEARCH, 17 December 2014.
[40] Interviews with officials from DG RESEARCH and BEPA, December 2014.
[41] Interview with an official from BEPA, 4 December 2014.
[42] Arnall 2003 (report commissioned by Greenpeace).

of the European Commission acted, despite its self-proclaimed rhetoric, as a tool to keep policy *insulated*, rather than open it. Invoking the participation of ethics experts in policy helped in making the claim that policy was more open, participatory and democratic, but in effect protected insulation.

Issue Technicalisation through Ethics Confinement

By limiting the mandate of the EGE to a narrow set of issues related to nanomedicine, EU policymakers were also able to avoid an 'ethics creep' to broader debates, such as those on toxicology and adequate regulation for nanoproducts – which it defined as non-ethical questions. The risk of an 'ethics creep' was avoided, essentially, by framing regulatory and ethical aspects as distinct and clearly separated matters.

Officials from DG RESEARCH or DG SANCO see safety and toxicology issues as technical in nature, and separate from ethical ones.[43] Talking about safety risks in nanomedicine, an official from DG RESEARCH stated that 'it is not about ethics', making it clear that 'on the one side we have safety risks, and on the other the ethics of societal engagement'.[44] Safety and toxicology concerns are portrayed as 'technical' and best solved through a cost-benefit type of analysis.[45] A member of the executive board of the ETP for Nanomedicine similarly explains that he 'would not regard safety as an ethical issue'. For him, ethical issues cover the questions of informed consent, the relationship between doctors and patients, human enhancement and issues of privacy with e-health. Safety and toxicology are, by contrast, 'more technical, cost-benefit types of issues'.[46] Ethics, thus, was perceived as encompassing a strictly delineated set of issues, which could better be dealt with through dialogue between policymakers and ethics experts. An official from DG RESEARCH explains that 'in nanomedicine the role of ethics was pretty clear ... so it was an obvious topic. This was something we could look at and ask meaningful questions about.'[47]

---

[43] Interviews with officials from DG RESEARCH and DG SANCO, 2014–2015.
[44] Interview with an official from DG RESEARCH, 23 June 2016.
[45] European Technology Platform for Nanomedicine 2005.
[46] Interview with a member of ETP for Nanomedicine, 30 June 2016.
[47] Interview with an official from DG RESEARCH, 17 December 2014.

Production and Mobilisation of Ethical Expertise 95

This distinction, confirmed by the EGE, enabled the Commission, in its communication on regulatory aspects of nanomaterials, to claim that 'it can be concluded that current legislation covers to a large extent risks in relation to nanomaterials and that risks can be dealt with under the current legislative framework'.[48] Similarly, though in a separate silo, 'ethical issues have to be dealt with, as indicated by the European Group on Ethics in Science and New Technologies'.[49] This established a clear division of labour between regulators and ethicists. By framing the most immediate and coherent safety concerns as laying beyond the realm of ethics, EU policy-makers steered the nanotechnology debate back into the technical arena. The pro-nanotechnology coalition succeeded in neutralising the ethical debate by disentangling ethical aspects from the regulatory realm, effectively technicalising the debate over nanomaterial regulation.

The Production of Ethics Expertise

Orchestration and ideational alignment were both at play throughout the process of knowledge production by expert bioethicists. *Orchestration* was clear in that EU policymakers directly transferred evidence to experts on the contours of the policy debate and the issue itself. Ideational alignment also occurred; experts and policymakers *interacted at various crossing points*, such as conferences, workshops or roundtables, where a common policy knowledge – common to experts and policymakers alike – was being developed.

EU policymakers clearly tried to orchestrate the process of knowledge production throughout the drafting of the EGE's opinion on nanomedicine. It was indeed much ahead of the Commission president's formal request for an opinion that the EGE experts participated in discussions on nanotechnologies that were taking place within the European Commission. Talking about the experts of the EGE, an official from DG RESEARCH explains that 'they had definitely been involved well before I arrived ... everyone in the Commission seemed to realise that they were there for a good reason and were playing an essential role, so everybody gave them time and answered their

[48] European Commission 2008a, p. 3.   [49] European Commission 2008a, p. 9.

questions. There was a well-established collaboration at that time already'.[50]

With the exception of EGE president Goran Hermeren, a Swedish professor of medical ethics, EGE members did not hold much expertise on nanotechnologies. Their limited knowledge gave considerable leeway to EU officials to influence them. Officials from all relevant DGs of the European Commission presented the position of their directorates to the EGE. The EGE, DG RESEARCH and DG SANCO therefore opened and sustained a dialogue on nanomedicine much in anticipation of the Commission president's formal request.

DG SANCO also worked in close collaboration with the EGE experts. In 2004, EGE members attended a workshop organised by the Risk Assessment Unit of DG SANCO, the objective of which was to develop a preliminary risk assessment of nanotechnology. In January 2006 when the experts were preparing their opinion, Philippe Martin from DG SANCO delivered to them a presentation on 'Health and Consumer Protection Considerations of Nanomedicine'. In his talk he argued that existing risk assessment procedures required modification for nanoparticles, but that the existing regulatory framework was adequate.[51] Philippe Martin's presentation left a lasting impression on ethics experts.[52] The EGE opinion on nanomedicine clearly follows DG SANCO's line of reasoning. An EGE expert confirms that the EGE's view was 'to use the existing regulatory framework until it had been demonstrated to be inadequate'.[53] In its opinion on nanomedicine, the EGE does not propose new regulatory structures, suggesting instead that changes be made within existing structures.[54] The general prognosis was clear: the potential benefits of moving ahead with nanoscience under existing regulatory frameworks outweighed the costs of a regulatory overhaul. The opinion of the EGE clearly echoed the Commission's position.

DG RESEARCH also presented material to the EGE during the opinion's drafting phase. In June 2006, Renzo Tomellini, then head of the Nanotechnology Unit in DG RESEARCH, delivered a presentation on 'Nanomedicine; success stories in FP6 and expectations in FP7' at an

---

[50] Interview with an official from DG RESEARCH, 17 December 2014.
[51] Archives of the EGE: http://ec.europa.eu/archives/european_group_ethics/archive/2005_2010/activities/docs/philippe_%20martin_final_en.pdf.
[52] Interviews with EGE members, April 2015.
[53] Interview with a member of EGE, 14 April 2015.
[54] European Group on Ethics 2007b, p. 57.

EGE work meeting.[55] The 'pro-nano' DGs of the European Commission *repeatedly interacted with ethics experts*, in an attempt to present to them the benefits of further developing nanotechnologies.

But the EGE experts were receptive interlocutors. Throughout the opinion's drafting phase they had worked together with EU policymakers – and, in the event, the industry. In December 2005, Dr Klaus Weltring, then leader of the ELSA board in the EU's funded Network of Excellence Nano2Life – which gathers together about 200 scientists as well as 'associate partners' from the nanotech industry – gave a talk to the EGE experts. He presented the mission of Nano2Life as that to 'improve European scientific excellence and industrial competitiveness in nanobiotech'.[56] He clearly laid out the potential benefits of nanotechnologies, with a particular focus on medical diagnostics, drug discovery and development, regenerative medicine, and neurosciences. Nano2Life's self-defined strategy consists in dressing up a 'state of the art' in the field of nanos, based on input from *scientists* and the *industry*. EGE members interacted with the members of the Nano2Life ELSA board while they were conducting their work. Scientists, nanotech companies, EU policymakers and the experts from the EGE all worked together so that a common policy knowledge emerged. Individuals also at times acted in various capacities and spanned roles. Klaus Weltring, for instance, became a member of the executive board of the ETP for Nanomedicine – an initiative led by industry – after having been involved with Nano2Life.

The roundtable organised by the EGE in March 2006 also acted as a crossing point between EU policymakers and experts. The EGE roundtable on 'The Ethical Aspects of Nanomedicine' was organised with the self-stated goal of promoting 'transparent dialogue with parties representing many different interests'.[57] But a closer examination of the participants in the discussion reveals that the roundtable included EGE experts, EU policymakers, scientists and representatives of religious groups in Europe. Representatives of consumers or 'Green' NGOs were not convened. Alzheimer Europe – which defends the voice of Alzheimer's patients in Europe – was the only civil society

---

[55] Archives of the EGE: https://ec.europa.eu/archives/european_group_ethics/archive/2005_2010/activities/docs/agenda_20_21_june2006_en.pdf.
[56] Weltring 2005.   [57] European Group on Ethics 2006.

association invited, and has a clear pro-nano position, hoping that nanomedicine may provide cures for neurodegenerative diseases.[58]

Recent Policy Moves

In February 2008, the European Commission adopted the Code of Conduct for Responsible Nanoscience and Nanotechnologies, which stresses the importance of 'anticipating potential environmental, health and safety impacts'.[59] The Code, however, essentially steers the self-regulation of nanotechnological business and research organisations – a key aspect of the European Commission's approach towards nanotechnologies, which can be seen as a tool to avoid regulatory reform, while still alleviating the potential fears of the public. For Janez Potočnik, then EU science and research commissioner, the Code 'is a tool developed by the Commission, ..., that will make it very simple to address the legitimate concerns that can arise regarding nanotechnologies'.[60]

Green MEPs, unconvinced by the European Commission's approach, have tried to push for stricter rules. The European Parliament's Committee on the Environment, Public Health and Food Safety (ENVI) tabled a motion for a resolution on the regulatory aspects of nanomaterials, drafted by Green MEP Carl Schlyter. The committee calls into question the Commission's reliance on 'a one-dimensional, legalistic overview of the current rules', which 'are about as effective in addressing nanotechnology as trying to catch plankton with a cod fishing net', and argues that 'stringent ethical guidelines need to be developed in due time, particularly for nanomedicine', arguing that both the environment and all consumers would benefit from regulation.[61] Ultimately, the committee argues, 'the likely convergence of nanotechnology with biotechnology, biology, cognitive sciences and information technology raises serious questions relating to ethics, safety, security and respect for fundamental rights that need to be analysed by a new opinion of the European Group on Ethics in Science and New Technologies'.[62] This move clearly signals the perceived policy leverage to be gained by re-invoking ethical expertise, with the EGE becoming a forum mobilised by each opposing coalition. The EGE, however, was not consulted again,

---

[58] European Group on Ethics 2006. [59] European Commission 2008b.
[60] CORDIS 2008. [61] European Parliament 2009.
[62] European Parliament 2009.

bringing further evidence that the EGE essentially works together with the European Commission.

Conclusion

Involving ethics experts in policymaking acted as a crucial element of the European Commission's broader 'anticipatory and integrated' approach and successfully contained the expansion of the conflict to the public at large. The moderate opposition that coalesced around the European Greens and their NGO counterparts could be defused and the push for nano-research took off – soon followed by the commercialisation of 'nano-products' in a number of consumption goods – from toothpaste to sun creams to candy.[63] EU policymakers had 'learned' from the GMO controversy that it is more convenient to anticipate protests than cope with them once they are well formulated and out there. The pro-science and innovation agenda of EU policymakers, articulated in a discourse on the potential of nanos for scientific progress and the EU's economic competitiveness, was made possible.

The mobilisation of ethics experts could help contain conflict because ethics expertise was produced in an iterative space between experts and policymakers. EU policymakers clearly attempted to 'orchestrate' the way ethics experts produced their knowledge, often by directly transferring their own evidence on nanotechnologies to them. But they did not need to do much because ideational alignment had already occurred. Bioethical knowledge was produced in crossing points – BEPA, conferences, workshops or roundtables – by a closed community of actors composed of EU policymakers, the industry and ethics experts, who came to share a similar way of seeing the problem at stake. As a result, the position of the EGE experts was stabilised and essentially echoed that of DG RESEARCH and DG SANCO, the two DGs most actively involved in nanotechnology policy.

The European Commission's anticipatory and integrated approach is surely anticipatory, in that it attempted to foresee any possible opposition, but it is less integrated than it claims. Since the invention

---

[63] See summary of research project from the French Institute for Agricultural Research (INRA): INRA 2017.

of synthetic material, nanotechnology is the only scientific development that unfolds the creation of *new material*, the health and environmental effects of which are still uncertain. Products containing nanoparticles have, however, been commercialised on a large scale, largely in the absence of genuine public debates in the media or elsewhere.

6 | *Tracking People's Behaviour*
From Conflict Containment to Conflict Manoeuvring

This chapter examines the production and mobilisation of ethical expertise in the case of data protection. In May 2011, the European Commission requested the EGE to issue two opinions on the ethics of information and communication technologies (ICTs). The involvement of ethics experts in the field of ICTs signalled a clear expansion of the mandate of the group beyond traditional bioethical issues. Two policy items shaped the context in which the European Commission mobilised the EGE. The first was the launch of the Digital Agenda by the Directorate General for Communications Networks, Content and Technology (DG CONNECT) of the European Commission. The second was the introduction, by DG RESEARCH, of sensitive security and defence areas in EU-funded research. The European Commission was concerned that both policy items would provoke opposition from civil society. As for nanotechnologies, EU officials mobilised ethics experts in order to check the rise of a potential policy conflict.

But while the EGE started working on the issue of data protection and privacy, another related policy reform became extremely controversial. Initiated by Viviane Reding, then EU Justice Commissioner, the general data protection reform, designed to promote a stricter regulation of data protection, provoked strong opposition from internet companies, the US government and other DGs within the European Commission. The conflict around the reform crystallised while the EGE was producing its two opinions, affecting both the reflections of the experts and the role they fulfilled in the policy process.

First, the EGE became a terrain of competition between several DGs of the European Commission involved in data protection issues. Each DG tried to present its own narrative of the policy problem to the EGE and orchestrate its work. The dominant pro-innovation narrative of

101

DG CONNECT and DG ENTR became contested by a pro-privacy narrative defended, in particular, by DG JUSTICE. In a context in which data privacy concerns gained ground in political debates, DG JUSTICE was able, at least temporarily, to recapture the debate and ensure that its concerns would be reflected in the EGE's first opinion.

Second, and as the competing narratives in place seemed increasingly irreconcilable, the EGE, in its second opinion, helped delineate a workable policy scenario. Ethics experts calibrated their findings in order to tame the controversy between the parties involved and provide policymakers with a more consensual narrative. As the politicisation of conflict became unavoidable, the role of ethics experts shifted from that of containing conflict to that of delineating a consensus and making policy possible. The pro-innovation narrative of EU policymakers, although clearly contested in the first EGE opinion, reappears in the second opinion of the group, testifying to its resilience in EU policy debates.

The Controversy over Data Protection

Launching the Digital Agenda: Lingering Fears over Big Data

In March 2010 the European Commission published its Europe 2020 strategy for smart, sustainable and inclusive growth, which lists the Digital Agenda as the first of its seven 'flagship initiatives' designed to get Europe 'back on track'.[1] Two months later it issued its communication *A Digital Agenda for Europe*, in which it explains that the objective of the Digital Agenda is 'to chart a course to maximise the social and economic potential of ICT'.[2] The Commission's proposals include, in particular, greater interoperability, improved internet infrastructure, wider access to digital technologies and ICT-related entrepreneurship and research. It also points to the need to build trust in the online environment by strengthening citizens' rights to privacy and data protection. But despite laudable goals on internet access and the boosting of ICT research, the Digital Agenda also includes more controversial policy proposals. While this appeared less clearly in early documents, from 2012 onwards DG CONNECT clearly supports policies

[1] European Commission 2010a.   [2] European Commission 2010b, p. 3.

favourable to so-called big data. Big data comes from voluminous digital datasets held by corporations, governments or other large organisations. These datasets can be analysed through computer algorithms, and used in a number of different sectors, such as healthcare, mobile communications, traffic management, fraud detection, and marketing and retail. From a commercial perspective, big data offers enormous potential benefits, and DG CONNECT clearly perceives its use as an economic driver in the EU. Here again, innovation and technological progress is clearly motivated by EU officials' belief that it will boost the EU's economic competitiveness.

This agenda can be traced back to the 2012 restructuring of the Directorate General for Information Society and Media (DG INFSO), which then became DG CONNECT. With the restructuring of the DG, a new Data Value Chain Unit, in charge of fostering commercial and social added value based on the use, management and reuse of data sources in Europe, was established. The key objectives of the unit consist in extracting value from data, which presupposes a wide availability of 'good-quality' data and the free flow of data across the EU. A new revenue model has indeed emerged for internet companies, which essentially relies on the tracking of online activity. The European Data Protection Supervisor (EDPS) itself has observed that 'the internet has evolved in a way that surveillance – tracking people's behaviour – is considered as the indispensable revenue model for some of the most successful companies'.[3] Big data is also perceived as a central resource for public authorities, which see it as a means to solve policy problems in a more efficient way and design better solutions for the future. In its 2014 communication *Towards a Thriving Data-Driven Economy*, the European Commission explains that 'analysing data means better results, processes and decisions' and 'helps us generate new ideas or solutions or to predict future events more accurately'.[4] Data analytics – which relies on the use of big data to analyse and predict – is perceived as a key resource for policymakers, as well as private companies.

Such developments, of course, do not come without some concerns. The European commission itself has recognised the drawbacks raised by the ease with which personal data has come to be shared and publicised in social networks, lamenting that 'the ways of collecting

---

[3] European Data Protection Supervisor 2015.
[4] European Commission 2014, p. 4.

personal data have become increasingly elaborated and less easily detectable'.[5] Citizens for their part increasingly perceive big data as a means to monitor human behaviour, either for purposes of consumer profiling, or for surveillance and control. Civil society associations have voiced concerns regarding personal data appropriation and control by data controllers.[6] In this context, DG CONNECT has become increasingly concerned about citizens' resistance to its policies, perceived as a potential obstacle to the smooth unfolding of its agenda, itself wrapped into a discourse on innovation and economic competitiveness.

The Data Protection Reform: Politicisation

While DG CONNECT was launching its Digital Agenda, the Directorate General for Justice, Fundamental Rights and Citizenship (DG JUSTICE) initiated another major reform, designed to revise the EU's legislative framework on data protection. Until 2010, both the European Commission and the Article 29 Data Protection Working Party, the advisory group on data protection and privacy,[7] argued that the regulatory framework in place was still adequate.[8] The Commission's agenda, however, took a new turn in 2010 with the appointment of Viviane Reding as commissioner for the newly created DG JUSTICE. Viviane Reding, formerly Commissioner for Information, Society and Media at the Directorate General for Information Society and Media (DG INFSO), had already advocated for more stringent policies on data protection and privacy, proposing, for instance, compulsory notifications of data breaches and consent requirements for data use in new technologies.[9] She had also initiated an inquiry into the UK's application of internet privacy laws while acting as Telecoms Commissioner.[10] Thus, as she took office as Justice Commissioner, she made it clear that data protection

---

[5] European Commission 2010c.
[6] European Digital Rights (EDRi), for instance, gathers together several NGOs which try to protect civil rights in the field of ICT.
[7] The group was composed of representatives of member states' data protection authorities, the EU data protection authority and a representative of the European Commission.
[8] Data protection was regulated by Directive 95/46/EC of 24 October 1995 on the protection of individuals with regard to the processing of personal data and on the free movement of such data.
[9] O'Brien 2009.   [10] Clark and Verkaik 2009.

The Controversy over Data Protection 105

would be a top priority for her. Addressing the European Parliament, she argued that although 'there can be no freedom without both security and justice ... during the past decade Europe's policies have too often focused only on security'. Referring to data protection, she also said that the privacy of European citizens should be strengthened in all European laws, expressing her scepticism that so many new restrictions were needed on peoples' privacy to fight terrorism.[11]

The proposed reform met with strong opposition within the European Commission. As DG JUSTICE was preparing the draft legislation, the European Commission was negotiating three personal data-related agreements with the United States: the agreement on the exchange of financial information under the Terrorist Finance Tracking Programme,[12] the Passenger Names Record (PNR) agreement, which concerned the exchange of passenger information, and finally an umbrella agreement for transfers of personal data between law enforcement authorities. DG HOME, which was negotiating these agreements with the United States and had a security-focused approach to data protection, quickly expressed its opposition to the reform package.[13] DG CONNECT and the Directorate General for Enterprise and Industry (DG ENTR) also expressed their concerns, although for different motives. For them, the new regulation threatened to impede the development of new web-based services and big data business models.[14]

After the draft text was leaked to the press in November 2011, internet companies such as Google and Facebook, the US Federal Trade Commission and some EU member states led by the UK engaged in intense lobbying activity.[15] The text planned to make European data protection rules applicable to all private and public actors, to data transfers with third countries, and to foreign-based companies whose data subjects were European citizens. It also included the 'right to be forgotten' for EU citizens, enabling them to delete personal information that they no longer wanted to share with banks, online booking

---

[11] European Parliament Hearing of Viviane Reding, 12 January 2010, http://ec.e uropa.eu/archives/commission%5F2010-2014/reding/pdf/mandate/reding%5F speaking%5Fpoints%5Fmedia%5Fsummary.pdf.
[12] The programme is also known as SWIFT (Society for Worldwide Interbank Financial Telecommunication).
[13] Interview with an assistant to an MEP, 3 December 2014.
[14] Interview with an official from DG Connect, 11 March 2015.
[15] Interview with an official from DG Justice, 2 December 2014.

websites or social media, and required that EU citizens give their 'explicit' consent before their data can be used. These proposals provoked an extraordinary degree of involvement in EU affairs on the part of the United States. Viviane Reding explained that American lobbyists simply 'tried to stop the Commission from putting legislation on the table' and that 'they tried to heavily intervene in Parliament, placing MEPs under enormous pressure'.[16] Companies, for their part, argued that a surfeit of regulations would prevent innovation and growth altogether. Facebook in particular had strong objections to the idea of a right to be forgotten, claiming that such a right raises concerns with regard to the right of others to remember and freedom of expression. In fact the data that Facebook users put on the site allows Facebook to publish targeted adverts – a chief source of the company's revenue. The US Federal Trade Commission actively supported these concerns and swiftly published an informal note criticising the draft text. The United States was particularly concerned about cross-border data transfers. During an official visit to the European Parliament in October 2012, representatives from the US Department of Commerce, as well as from the US Department of Justice, openly criticised the reform plans. The former argued that it would hurt the economy and cost jobs, while the latter stated it would pose a security threat.[17] Quite a diverse set of actors – either out of *security*, or *economic* concerns – coalesced against a stricter protection of privacy.

Privacy and civil rights associations strongly supported the draft text, and denounced the interference from lobbies, lamenting that they had succeeded in watering down some of the provisions of the draft regulation before it was even published officially. The note from the US Federal Trade Commission indeed pushed several Commission services to issue negative internal opinions before the final draft was revealed.[18] In particular, a provision that prevented European data controllers from directly handling over data at the request of a third country government or court, but only through existing data cooperation agreements at the member-state or EU level, was withdrawn from the text. The US government, as well as DG HOME within the European Commission, had strongly resisted this provision.[19] The

[16] Cited in Levy-Abegnoli 2016.
[17] 'Paper sees Germany, EU, USA at odds over plan for EU-wide data privacy standards' 2012.
[18] EDRi 2012. [19] Interview with an assistant to an MEP, 3 December 2014.

prescribed fines for violations of data protection (by any company working in the EU or treating EU citizens' data) were also lower than in the first proposals issued by Commissioner Reding.

When the legislative process moved forward and the text was transferred to the European Parliament, the latter clearly supported the reform. Although the European Commission produced two separate proposals, for a regulation on data protection reform and for a directive on police and judicial cooperation, the parliament followed a 'single package' treatment for both pieces.[20] In November 2013, MEP Dimitrios Droutsas, rapporteur for the directive on police and judicial cooperation, presented a report introducing substantial amendments to the original text, with the purpose of raising the standards of protection to a level similar to those of the proposed regulation.[21] At the same time, Green MEP Jan Philipp Albrecht, rapporteur for the regulation, issued a report tightening the original provisions of the Commission draft regulation on consent requirements, individual rights and accountability obligations.[22] In March 2014, the Parliament voted for the regulation almost unanimously in the first reading. The directive on police and judicial cooperation passed by a smaller margin (371 votes in favour, 276 against and 20 abstentions).[23]

But debates went on within the Council which, by the time the package was approved by the Parliament, had not managed to secure an agreement. The British government was hostile to the new legislation, considering it too rigid, costly and cumbersome for companies. The UK Information Commissioner (the national data protection authority) expressed its scepticism that the right to be forgotten could be implemented at all.[24] The Netherlands and Denmark echoed these concerns. Germany had a more ambiguous position. While the then minister of interior Hans-Peter Friedrich opposed the draft, Consumer Protection Minister Ilse Aigner supported it and criticised internet companies like Facebook and Google for their lobbying campaigns.[25]

---

[20] See European Parliament debates of 21 November 2012, www.europarl.europa.eu/sides/getDoc.do?pubRef=-//EP//TEXT+CRE+20121121+ITEM-016+DOC+XML+V0//EN.
[21] European Parliament 2012. [22] European Parliament 2013.
[23] European Parliament Legislative Observatory, Final Vote 12/03/2014: www.europarl.europa.eu/oeil/popups/sda.do?id=23715%26l=en.
[24] 'UK reacts to Google "right to be forgotten" ruling' 2014.
[25] 'Paper sees Germany, EU, USA at odds over plan for EU-wide data privacy standards' 2012.

After taking office in late 2013, the new German minister of the interior backed the reform within the Council.

It was, thus, in the context of a highly politicised debate that the European Commission mobilised the EGE. On the one hand, DG CONNECT was trying to pursue the launch of its Digital Agenda and feared reactions from civil society associations. In 2011, when President Barroso formally requested the EGE to issue its opinions on ICTs, this was the central concern of the European Commission. On the other, DG JUSTICE pushed for a stricter regulation of data protection through the general data protection reform, provoking fierce opposition from internet companies, the US government and other DGs preoccupied with security and surveillance within the European Commission. The political context of the data protection reform and the internal competition *amongst* the DGs of the European Commission strongly impacted on the work of the EGE experts.

Production and Mobilisation of Ethical Expertise

In March 2011, President Manuel Barroso officially requested the EGE to produce two opinions on the ethics of ICTs. His letter to the EGE stated that the first opinion would act as 'a reference point to the Commission to promote a responsible use of the Digital Agenda for Europe and facilitate the societal acceptance of such an important policy item'.[26] He then asked the EGE to issue a second opinion focusing more specifically on the ethical implications of ICT research related to security technologies under FP7, which 'may offer a reference point to the Commission to promote responsible use of security technologies and policies in FP7 and facilitate the social acceptance of such an important policy area'.[27]

Pre-empting Conflict

Specific DGs were at the origin of the President's request. DG CONNECT and DG ENTR were most interested in having the EGE produce the first general opinion on ICTs. DG RESEARCH was, for its part, interested in having an EGE opinion on funding research on ICT technologies related to defence and security. An expert from the EGE

[26] Barroso 2011.   [27] Barroso 2011.

explains that 'the request to our group was not made out of the blue; we had conversations over years with the European Commission', adding that 'the formal procedure hides the consultations beforehand'.[28]

DG CONNECT was responsible for the launch of the Digital Agenda, and was naturally the DG most closely involved with data protection issues. By involving ethics experts in the policy process, DG CONNECT hoped to tackle potential social and ethical concerns in a way that would not hamper the launch of the Digital Agenda. In the words of a DG CONNECT official, Commissioner Neelie Kroes wanted 'to show how to make existing policies evolve in a proactive fashion, and not in a reactive manner which would block innovation'.[29] In this context DG CONNECT wanted 'to prevent the polarisation of the debate, as had happened in other issue areas such as nuclear energy or GMOs'.[30] Neelie Kroes was concerned, in particular, that civil society organisations, which had expressed their concerns about the production and use of big data, may block the Digital Agenda. DG ENTR had similar concerns. It hoped that the EGE opinion would allow for the inclusion of social concerns in a fashion that would not go against the interests of enterprises.[31] It also expected that the EGE opinion would prevent a polarisation of the debate, between the advocates of a strict protection of privacy and those who defend the need for enterprises to make profit. An official from DG CONNECT explained well that: 'We wanted a framework that would allow the development of connected services. And everyone wanted to move ahead in a way that is satisfying for both society and industry. We wanted to avoid reactions concerning big data'.[32]

For DG CONNECT and DG ENTR, the mobilisation of ethics experts was perceived as a conflict containment mechanism. The two DGs feared that citizens may protest against reforms perceived as promoting the use of big data, and tried to ensure that policy remained formulated within a closed community. Making the claim that ethical issues had been tackled and solved by ethics experts in fact helped them to do this.

---

[28] Interview with a member of the EGE, 27 March 2015.
[29] Interview with an official from DG Connect, 11 March 2015.
[30] Interview with an official from DG Connect, 11 March 2015.
[31] Interview with an official from DG Connect, 2 March 2016.
[32] Interview with an official from DG Connect, 2 March 2016.

For the second EGE opinion focusing specifically on the ethical implications of security technologies in research funded by the EU, EU policymakers were particularly concerned about developments in biosecurity and cybersecurity. This concern surfaced with the inclusion of security and defence technologies in EU research programmes.[33] President Barroso suggested that the EGE provide 'an analysis on how to further embed ethics into security technologies'.[34] Specific security applications such as internet profiling, body scans, the use of different bio-identification tools (such as fingerprinting, chips inserted into humans, etc.), biometrics and other ICT surveillance methods were at stake.[35] These technologies foreshadowed the raising of new concerns amongst EU citizens, and the European Commission wanted to pre-empt opposition to such technological applications. By involving experts in policymaking, the European Commission hoped to check the rise of a potential conflict on these issues too.

As the work of the EGE moved on, however, the legislative reform on data protection launched by DG JUSTICE had become divisive. In the words of an EGE member, the 'ICT domain became more and more controversial because of big data and privacy issues that it implied'.[36] One of the rapporteurs for the EGE opinion also explains that data protection was considered 'a major issue on the highest level in the European Commission'.[37] The EGE therefore found itself working on the issue of data protection in a highly politicised context.

Opinion 26 on the Ethics of Information and Communication Technologies

Producing Knowledge: Ideational Alignment Makes Orchestration Trouble-Free

The involvement of the EGE with the ethics of ICTs signalled a clear and unexpected expansion of its mandate beyond classic bioethical issues. EGE experts who were trained in medicine, bioethics, biotechnology or law, did not have expertise in the field of ICTs. The fact that

---

[33] Interview with a member of the EGE, 23 December 2015.   [34] Barroso 2011.
[35] Interview with a member of the EGE, 23 December 2015.
[36] Interview with a member of the EGE, 12 November 2015.
[37] Interview with one of the rapporteurs for Opinion 26 in the EGE, 27 March 2015.

they were not specialists in the field had a clear impact on the way they worked in producing the two opinions. Most of them felt that the issue was new to them.[38] As a result, 'the first step consisted in being widely informed'[39] and the EGE essentially relied on external information in order to produce its opinions on ICT issues. Members of several DGs presented their views to the EGE experts during this preparatory phase. The EGE also held several hearings with external experts. Between March 2011 and February 2012, when its first opinion on ICTs was issued, the EGE held ten meetings with representatives of the European Commission and academic experts. In a first stage, members of the cabinet of DG INFSO[40] presented their views to the group. At the first hearings in April 2012, two officials from DG INFSO gave a presentation to the EGE.[41] But as the work of the EGE moved on, members of Viviane Reding's cabinet started to become involved. At its June 2012 hearings, Jan Ostoja-Ostaszewski from Viviane Reding's cabinet, as well as Giovanni Buttarelli, then deputy EU data protection supervisor, also gave a talk to the EGE.[42] The EGE relied heavily on evidence transferred by the European Commission, which it was meant to advise. Evidence transfers were particularly patent in the case of ICTs, because of experts' lack of prior knowledge in the field. As the EGE experts moved on with their work, it is clear that DG JUSTICE, which had launched the data protection reform, tried to 'recapture' the EGE's work and ensure that the EGE opinions would also include its preferences.

Moreover, the EGE and the European Commission also worked closely together in various crossing points. In November 2011, the EGE hosted a large roundtable which acted as an arena.[43] Academics, representatives of big companies such as Google and Telefonica, representatives of the civil society, and members of the European Commission and of other international institutions, were all convened. Invited speakers included Fabrizio Sestini from DG INFSO, as well as Peter Hustinx, the European data protection

---

[38] Interview with a member of the EGE, 12 November 2015.
[39] Interview with a member of the EGE, 24 August 2015.
[40] At the time DG Connect was still called DG INFSO.
[41] Bureau of European Policy Advisers (BEPA) 2014.
[42] Bureau of European Policy Advisers (BEPA) 2014.
[43] Archives from the EGE: http://ec.europa.eu/archives/bepa/european-group-ethics/docs/activities/press_release_ege_round_table_on_ict_29.11.11.pdf.

supervisor. The Bureau of European Policy Advisors (BEPA) also acted as a vector between the EGE and the European Commission. EGE experts, Commission officials and academic experts worked closely together through BEPA. Through all these iterations, the DGs of the European Commission were able to talk with the EGE experts and present their views to them. A new phenomenon occurred, via which different DGs *competed* for the EGE's attention and the experts group became a lobbying terrain.

The Recapture of Ethics Experts by DG JUSTICE

As the EGE experts moved on with their work, DG JUSTICE increasingly interacted with them. Commissioner Viviane Reding was particularly interested in promoting her proposals on issues such as privacy and the 'right to be forgotten'.[44] She repeatedly expressed her support for the 'right to be forgotten', explaining that 'if an individual no longer wants his personal data to be processed or stored by a data controller, and if there is no legitimate reason for keeping it, the data should be removed'.[45] In another speech, she stressed that individuals 'should be able to maintain control over their data' and that 'the right to be forgotten is particularly relevant to personal data that is no longer needed for the purposes for which it was collected'.[46]

In February 2012, the EGE adopted its Opinion 26, 'Ethics of Information and Communication Technologies'.[47] The opinion strongly echoes with the concerns of DG JUSTICE concerning privacy issues. It does so by placing ICT issues into a broader philosophical and sociological context and alerting against the dangers that ICTs may cause to our private sphere. In the preamble of the opinion, the EGE explains that 'aware of the changes that have come about in the lives of most citizens of the European Union, and further afield, as a result of the pervasiveness of new electronic media, the challenge is to ensure that the availability of electronic information and the use of ICT are handled in an ethical manner'.[48] The EGE engages with the concept of identity in the digital era, referring to Paul Ricoeur's *Oneself as Another* (1995), and *Liquid Life* by Zygmunt Bauman (2005), who

---

[44] Interview with a member of the EGE, 24 February 2015. [45] Reding 2012.
[46] Reding 2010. [47] European Group on Ethics 2012.
[48] European Group on Ethics 2012, p. 14.

Ethics of Information and Communication Technologies 113

has discussed the fluidity of modern social relations. When the opinion moves to the more specific discussion of privacy as a fundamental right, the group evokes Hannah Arendt's work, arguing that 'Arendt's defence of the importance of the private sphere warns about dangers arising from the erosion of the private, a situation which some consider as deriving from the use of ICT as communication tools'.[49]

The more specific recommendations from the EGE focus on ensuring transparency, guaranteeing informed consent and withdrawal of it, and additional safeguards for children and vulnerable adults. The EGE extensively builds on the European Commission's policy proposals on data protection, as well as the opinions of the European Data Supervisor, in particular concerning the issue of consent for processing information and the right to withdraw it.[50] Its opinion directly quotes the Commission's proposals, essentially drafted by DG JUSTICE, stating that 'it is time to build a stronger and more coherent data protection framework in the EU', which will 'put individuals in control of their own data and reinforce legal and practical certainty for economic operators and public authorities'.[51]

The EGE states, first, that 'any person should have a 'right to be forgotten''.[52] The group's recommendations on the right to be forgotten fully echo Viviane Reding's preferences. The opinion then supports greater transparency on the part of data controllers, by arguing that it is 'essential that individuals should be well and clearly informed, in a transparent way, by data controllers about how and by whom their data are collected and processed, for what reasons, for how long, how it will be shared with others and what their rights are if they want to access, rectify or delete their data'.[53] The EGE also supports the right for individuals to withdraw their consent to the processing of data. Ultimately ethics experts largely echoed views from DG JUSTICE. Testifying to this, the officials from DG CONNECT expressed their disquiet about the content of the EGE opinion. In the words of a DG CONNECT official, the EGE remained locked in 'dated modes of thinking' and did not adjust to the new circumstances triggered by technological developments.[54] In the face of the counter-narrative presented by

---

[49] European Group on Ethics 2012, p. 44.
[50] European Group on Ethics 2012, pp. 45–8.
[51] European Group on Ethics 2012, p. 45.
[52] European Group on Ethics 2012, p. 48.
[53] European Group on Ethics 2012, p. 47.
[54] Interview with a member of the EGE, 2 March 2016.

DG JUSTICE, DG CONNECT presented it as not up to date and not sufficiently pro-innovation.

Thus, although DG ENTR and DG CONNECT were behind President Barroso's initiative to involve the EGE, DG JUSTICE recaptured the discussions with the experts once their work got under way. Viviane Reding and her cabinet presented their own concerns and way of looking at data protection problems to the experts. Ethics experts were sensitive to the arguments from DG JUSTICE, which echoed their own concerns on the need for some degree of protection for personal data. As explained by one of the opinion rapporteurs, members of the EGE 'wanted to protect privacy; lots of people wanted this but this was also our opinion'.[55] Ethics experts have given support to those who were in support of privacy at a time when such arguments gained significant ground in EU debates.

Ethics of Security and Surveillance Technologies

The story for the second EGE opinion on the ethical implications of security technologies is quite a different one. Although the European Commission's initial concern was the use of security technologies under FP7, the focus of the opinion drifted towards the question of surveillance in the context of the Snowden policy crisis. In this move, the EGE switched back to its focus on data protection and privacy, but did so in a context that was ignited by the Snowden revelations. The role of ethics experts, in this context, shifted to that of *conflict taming* through the articulation, in particular, of a rhetoric designed to articulate a link between existing narratives.

Orchestration

Immediately after the request from President Barroso, the EGE started its work on the ethical implications of security technologies. In a similar way as for its work on Opinion 26, it worked in collaboration with EU officials – in particular from DG RESEARCH, responsible for the EU's framework programmes – and BEPA. In July 2011, the French Institute for Higher National Defence Studies co-organised, together with BEPA, a conference on 'Common Security and Defense Policy, Ethics

---

[55] Interview with a member of the EGE, 24 August 2015.

and Moral Values' in Brussels. Amongst a number of high-profile experts, Jean-Claude Thebault, then director general of BEPA, as well as Professor Linda Nielsen, EGE rapporteur for Opinion 28, both took part to the conference.[56] In September the same year, the EGE and the EU National Ethics Councils Forum (NEC Forum), which gathers representatives of the National Ethics Councils of EU states, also met in Brussels. The Joint EGE–NEC Forum meeting was again organised by BEPA in collaboration with DG RESEARCH. In a similar fashion as for Opinion 26, the EGE worked in close collaboration with policymakers when drafting its opinion.

The work of the EGE on Opinion 28 was, however, interrupted by an unforeseen request from the European Commission that the EGE works on the ethics of energy. As a result, it was only in February 2013 that the EGE officially resumed its work on Opinion 28. At the time security concerns were still at the core of the EGE's focus and its members continued to gain knowledge of the security and defence issues that were of concern to DG RESEARCH. During its first work meeting on the issue in March 2013, the EGE hosted a number of speakers. Christoph Kautz, from DG ENTR, as well as Dorian Karatzas from DG RESEARCH, gave a talk on security and ethics in FP7 projects. Dr Anna Lönnroth from DG RESEARCH also spoke to the group about the ethical safety and security considerations around the funding of gain-of-function research in infectious diseases, which includes potentially risky experiments in virology aimed at understanding the biology, ecology and pathogenesis of viruses.[57] Clearly, discussions centred around security issues in research policy. During this first phase of the EGE's work, DG RESEARCH transferred evidence to the EGE experts, informing them about policy-relevant issues and how to approach them. While the experts are free to use, or not, such evidence, the fact that EU policymakers were their main source of information led to a process of knowledge production that was heavily orchestrated by EU officials.

The Snowden Crisis: The Shift towards Surveillance

From June 2013 onwards, discussions inside the EGE shifted towards the issue of surveillance. A political crisis, provoked by revelations that

---

[56] Bureau of European Policy Advisers (BEPA) 2014.
[57] Bureau of European Policy Advisers (BEPA) 2014.

the United States was engaged in massive surveillance activities, shifted discussions back to the issue of surveillance. In June 2013, the press published evidence of mass surveillance activities by the US government.[58] US citizen Edward Snowden, who then worked as a contractor for the US National Security Agency (NSA), leaked classified information revealing the existence of the PRISM programme, launched by the NSA in 2007.[59] The Snowden revelations produced an unexpected turn in the production process of the EGE opinion. Discussions shifted in focus, from the funding of security technologies under FP7 to the issue of surveillance.[60] EGE experts had not ignored surveillance questions formerly, but with the Snowden revelations, the issue took centre stage. In Opinion 28, 'Ethics of Security and Surveillance Technologies', which was adopted in June 2014, the EGE acknowledged that the Snowden revelations made it important to reinterpret the EU's approach to surveillance and security.[61]

After the discussion switched towards surveillance issues, Viviane Reding and her cabinet became actively involved in the drafting process of Opinion 28.[62] An official from DG JUSTICE, for instance, explained that he 'held a session with the group and talked about trade-offs, the risks of technology, and in particular what risks there could be if surveillance was left unchecked'.[63] Viviane Reding used the momentum of the crisis to openly criticise the sluggish progress in approving the data protection reform, singling out the heads of state who had shown support for the reform in an October 2013 gathering (i.e. the French president and the Polish and Italian prime ministers) while accusing the others of surrendering to 'the spin of lobbyists'. In her view, the text was ready to be approved as soon as there was 'political will to do so'.[64] The Snowden crisis provided DG JUSTICE with an ideal window of opportunity to push for its proposals. In the highly politicised context of the data protection reform, which got ignited by the Snowden revelations, civil society organisations were also

---

[58] See, for instance, Gleenwald 2013.
[59] PRISM is the code name for the programme under which the NSA collects internet communications from various US internet companies.
[60] Interview with a member of the EGE, 23 December 2015.
[61] European Group on Ethics 2014, p. 13.
[62] Interview with a member of the EGE, 23 December 2015.
[63] Interview with an official from DG Justice, European Commission, 13 August 2017.
[64] Reding 2014.

increasingly active and resisted what they saw as intrusions on individuals' privacy.

All these protests agitated other units of the European Commission. DG HOME, for security concerns, and DG CONNECT together with DG ENTR, for economic concerns, all pushed for a more lenient protection of privacy. DG CONNECT and DG ENTR were concerned about the polarisation of the debate between, on the one hand, the industry preoccupied with furthering its profits and, on the other, civil society organisations expressing their opposition in a reactionary manner. In this context it became important for DG ENTR to include societal issues in a 'non-reactionary, non-activist, anti-industry mode'. Officials from DG ENTR thus hoped that the EGE opinion 'would convince people that we could let enterprises do their work'.[65] DG HOME was still concerned about the tracking of criminal activities. As the policy debate became increasingly polarised, the competing DGs of the European Commission kept interacting with the EGE experts. By then DG CONNECT and DG ENTR had realised the opportunity to also develop interactions with the EGE and pull their weight in the work of ethics experts.

Knowledge Calibration

In May 2014, the EGE issued its opinion. It includes concerns voiced by different DGs of the European Commission. But EGE experts essentially deconstructed binary oppositions that were voiced in ongoing debates over privacy, crafting a rhetoric which was capable of reframing existing narratives. Thus, the EGE claims to be moving beyond the 'trade-off' narrative, arguing that it constitutes a 'misleading framework'.[66] The experts criticise what they see as a 'limited approach to achieving security, most especially when it comes to the narrow interpretation of state security' which has consisted in 'engaging in the narrative of trade-offs, the classic example being the trade-off between freedom, often embodied as privacy, and security'.[67]

Calibrating its knowledge output, the recommendations of the EGE carefully include concerns from different DGs of the European

---

[65] Interview with an official from DG Connect, 2 March 2016.
[66] European Group on Ethics 2014, p. 84.
[67] European Group on Ethics 2014, p. 87.

Commission. Some of its recommendations are in line with the position of DG JUSTICE. The EGE states that the Entry/Exit System (EES) proposed under the Smart Borders Initiative involves a disproportionate intrusion into individuals' privacy and recommends a moratorium on the introduction of the EES.[68] For one of the rapporteurs for Opinion 28, the opinion was important because 'European policymakers needed solid arguments in security issues. They wanted to argue for more privacy'.[69] The EGE also states that the power to have people under surveillance should be strictly delineated: it should be granted only for specific purposes and for a defined period of time. Concerning the issue of big data, the EGE recommends that the 'profiling of individuals for commercial purposes should be subject to the individual's explicit consent'.[70] It also expresses its concern that 'without proper attention, the principle of purpose limitation at the core of data protection will be undermined' and that as far as possible data should be anonymised.[71] Other than this, it limits itself to suggesting that 'the EU develops a code of conduct for Big Data analytics that would guide organisations with the process'.[72] Thus, the opinion echoes some of the concerns of DG JUSTICE. This is not very surprising, given the iterations between the members of the DG and the EGE throughout the writing of the opinion.

But important aspects of the EGE's recommendations are more in line with the preferences of DG CONNECT and DG ENTR, showing that the dominant 'pro-innovation' narrative is hard to contest. The EGE puts the principles of effectiveness and proportionality at the core of its reasoning – an approach strongly favoured by the industry.[73] Arguing that it is necessary to 'move beyond the rhetoric of trade-offs', the EGE proposes that security technologies and measures are assessed on the basis of proportionality and effectiveness, and rights are prioritised, rather than traded. It further states that surveillance 'must be necessary and proportionate in order to ensure an appropriate connection between the actions taken and the objectives achieved'.[74] The EGE suggests the use of privacy impact assessment (PIA) procedures when

---

[68] European Group on Ethics 2014, p. 90.
[69] Interview with a member of the EGE, 24 August 2015.
[70] European Group on Ethics 2014, p. 89.
[71] European Group on Ethics 2014, p. 90.
[72] European Group on Ethics 2014, p. 90.   [73] Digital Europe 2015.
[74] European Group on Ethics 2014, p. 87.

new information systems that process personal data are being introduced to the market in order to evaluate the potential implications of the proposed technology for personal data. In this second opinion, the experts prioritised the construction of a discourse integrating conflicting views but also deconstructing what it presented as a rhetoric of trade-offs between opposed objectives. Experts calibrated their opinion in order to present an output that was simply *acceptable* to the policy actors in place and which could also *make policy possible* by providing policymakers with a reconciling discourse.

Recent Policy Moves: The Adoption of the EU Data Protection Regulation

Following four years of intense negotiations, the EU's General Data Protection Regulation (EDPR) was adopted in April 2016, together with the Law Enforcement Data Protection Directive (LEDP), which covers processing of personal data by law enforcement authorities.[75] The Snowden crisis was instrumental in strengthening consensus around the reform, not least from heads of state such as Angela Merkel.[76]

The EDPR includes the right to be forgotten (relabelled right of erasure), so important to DG JUSTICE. It also includes provisions on clear and affirmative consent, children on social media, and the right for individuals to know when their data has been hacked. It also stipulates that companies that breach these rules can face steep fines, up to 4 per cent of their global turnover. Crucially, the regulation's scope applies to companies outside Europe, such as those in the United States that offer goods and services to Europeans and which can now face the same penalties for non-compliance with EU rules.

But the regulation also promotes a risk-based approach to data protection, strongly advocated by the digital industry. For instance, Digital Europe – which represents some of the world's largest IT, telecoms and consumer electronics companies – made it clear that risk needs to be the predominant consideration in determining how personal data is adequately protected without imposing inappropriate

---

[75] European Parliament and Council 2016a, 2016b.
[76] Interview with an assistant to a MEP, 3 December 2014.

or disproportionate burdens.[77] Two legal tools in particular give significant discretion to data controllers or processors. First, data protection impact assessments should be carried out by data controllers 'prior to risky processing operations' only when data processing presents 'high risks' for the rights and freedoms of citizens.[78] Second, the regulation includes a clause on the prevention of ex-post misuse of data through prompt notification of data breaches, but such notifications are left to the responsibility of data controllers.[79] The regulation also enshrines the principle of data protection by design – when the attentive implementation of data protection principles is embedded in the design of a new technology. But a closer reading of the provisions of the regulation reveals potential weaknesses in the approach. The regulation forces data controllers to think about data protection when developing data-driven technologies, and to 'implement appropriate technical and organisational measures'.[80] However, besides mentioning pseudonymisation as an appropriate technique, no clear standards are brought forward. The regulation in fact remains largely in line with the interests of EU digital companies. By contrast, privacy associations were disappointed with the final content of the regulation and felt that they were not able to push for their own narrative. Joe McNamee, executive director of European Digital Rights, commented that 'much of the ambition of the original data protection package was lost, due to one of the biggest lobbying campaigns in European history'.[81] The new regulatory regime essentially promotes the interests of EU digital companies against those of US companies, which did not have to submit to EU rules under the former regime, but it does not challenge the EU's pro-innovation narrative. This explains the fierce lobbying campaigns of US internet companies, as well as the US government, which repeatedly invoked security concerns in order to prevent the adoption of the regulation. In December 2015, US Attorney General Loretta Lynch, for instance, warned that the planned regulation could undermine efforts to thwart terrorist attacks by restricting transatlantic information sharing.[82]

---

[77] Digital Europe 2013.   [78] European Parliament and Council 2016a.
[79] European Parliament and Council 2016a. See also Gonçalves 2017 for a full analysis of these aspects of the regulation.
[80] European Parliament and Council 2016a, Article 25.   [81] McNamee 2016.
[82] See Wilhelm 2020.

Conclusions

Both for the first and for the second opinion on ICTs, the European Commission mobilised the EGE in order to *contain potential conflicts* related to the launch of the Digital Agenda and the funding of sensitive defence and security technologies under FP7. But the politicisation of the debate that occurred with the launch of the data protection reform resulted in a greater interest in the activities of the EGE on the part of different DGs. The expert group became a new *locus* where the different units of the European Commission pushed for their competing narratives. For the first opinion, DG JUSTICE was able to orchestrate the reflections of the group, perhaps because its arguments resonated well with the preoccupations of the experts, but also because it actively interacted with them. For the second opinion, DG CONNECT and DG ENTR were more wary of letting the EGE terrain to DG JUSTICE and intervened actively too. In this context, the function of the experts in the policy process shifted from that of containing to that of managing conflict. In a smart rhetorical exercise, ethics experts provided policymakers with a discourse that framed arguments presented until then as strictly opposed and incompatible, as reconcilable.

The case of data protection indicates that ethics experts are involved in an increasingly large number of policy domains, which go far beyond the typical bioethical issues of the 1990s, such as human experimentation and questions associated with the beginning and end of life. Data protection is not part of the traditional territory of ethics experts and their involvement in this domain signals that resorting to 'ethics' – an expert discourse on ethics – is considered increasingly useful by policymakers who want to push for certain scientific or technological reforms. Calibration, orchestration and ideational alignment all operated at different points of the policy process. Because EU policymakers defended competing narratives, the position of ethics experts also fluctuated between the two discourses, leaving the experts to eventually calibrate their claims in order to delineate a more consensual discourse which would make policy possible.

7 Conclusion

The Politics of Expertising Ethics

This book reveals that the emergence, production and mobilisation of ethical expertise by policymakers is political. Involving ethics experts in policy fulfils a complex role in the governance of scientific and technological innovation. The mobilisation of 'ethics experts' does not only arise from a motivation to 'know better', and neither does it only provide legitimacy to certain political agendas.[1] Involving ethics experts in policy can help policymakers manoeuvre though potential or existing policy conflicts over scientific and technological innovations. In doing so, the mobilisation of ethical expertise acts as a stabilisation mechanism for the dominant pro-science and innovation narrative. Bioethical expertise can be mobilised as a mechanism that helps to contain conflict, as evidenced by the case of nanotechnology policy. It can also, when a controversy has already arisen, help policymakers bypass the conflict and find closure in the expert arena. This was well evidenced in the case of human embryonic stem cell research. It was to some extent also evidenced in the data protection case, where ethics experts provided policymakers with a reconciling rhetoric and helped them tame the policy conflict that had exploded in the context of the data protection reform. The mobilisation of ethical expertise, although presented as an inclusive and deliberative mechanism, in fact acted as a way of insulating policy, depoliticising issues and facilitating the closing of controversies. Policymakers were able to mobilise ethics experts to such avail because the emergence and the production of bioethical expertise did not take place independently from politics.

The very creation of bioethics as an expert discourse was indeed enmeshed with politics. Its tenets are compatible with a pro-science and

---

[1] See, for instance, Salter 2007; Plomer 2008.

market-oriented framing of scientific and technological issues. Mainstream bioethics is dominated by utilitarian considerations, based on balancing risks and benefits, and does not contain the possibility of contesting the dominant pro-innovation and market-friendly narrative which informs policies on scientific and technological innovation. It embodies a particular way of knowing things, which in turn shapes the contours of how new technologies are evaluated and acted upon.

Although bioethics as an expert discourse has been contested by non-expert voices who claim a voice in the debate or within the expert sphere itself, this book reveals that three logics of iteration between experts and policymakers, which I labelled orchestration, ideational alignment and calibration, act as mechanisms of *stabilisation* of the content and form of ethical expertise. First, policymakers engage in tactics to *orchestrate* the process of knowledge production, to ensure that bioethicists do not diverge from their own pro-innovation and pro-market stance. They deploy various strategies to that effect. They pick and choose certain experts and leave others aside, frame experts' discussions, transfer evidence to them, explain what solutions seem 'acceptable' and even discuss with them the substance of the issue at stake. The unilaterality of this logic, however, is diluted because other iteration mechanisms are at play. Policymakers often find experts to be very receptive interlocutors, because their thinking is already *ideationally aligned* with ongoing policy debates and narratives. It is the participation of experts and policymakers at crossing points – those spaces where policymakers and scientists meet, talk and deliberate – that induces the production of approaches to policy problems which become common to experts and policymakers alike. On the other hand, experts can themselves *calibrate* the knowledge they produce, in order to adjust it to the needs of a given policy debate. And when policymakers disagree amongst themselves – as in the case of data protection – expert groups can also become a terrain of competition for policymakers with divergent preferences. Here experts are under increased pressure to calibrate their claims to propose a policy solution acceptable to all. Because these three logics of iteration are at play, the mobilisation of bioethical expertise allows policymakers to manoeuvre through conflicts and ultimately *makes policy possible*. Bioethics as an expert discourse acts as a stabilisation mechanism in the management of scientific and technological governance.

Ethics expertise is political, in its production and mobilisation, and yet it is mobilised as an apolitical, neutral or universal set of concepts supposed to be guiding political action. The emergence, back in the 1970s, of principlism – an essentially utilitarian framework – as a dominant bioethics doctrine has enabled bioethics to claim a degree of neutrality between substantive approaches. Ethics experts take great care to present themselves as 'independent', 'objective' and 'neutral' possessors of specialist, academic knowledge. The emergence of ethics expertise has led to the development of specific forms of reasoning and concepts and the invention of a unique terminology that make these claims to impartiality easier. The framing of ethics as an *expert issue* has reinforced the indisputability of decisions that have 'passed' the test of ethics approval. The making of a new class of experts, who claim to have the capacity to deliberate on the values at stake in biomedical research and scientific advances, has also contributed to the exclusion of various non-expert voices from debates on scientific and technological innovations. In particular, it has delegitimised claims that citizens themselves, lay patients and consumers should have their say on such issues. It has in fact taken issues that have an explicit ethical component out of the realm of democratic debate.

Recent contributions in IR have revealed that policymakers invoke 'ethics' as a pure set of principles, separated from politics, which can guide us towards a better world not tainted by politics.[2] Zehfuss in her book on 'ethical war', for instance, argues that because ethics is construed as distinct from politics, such decisions are removed from the realm of political debate and contestation.[3] Fagan also points to the way policymakers employ the category of ethics in order to depoliticise issues and contain the opening up of political debates. Ethics, she claims, is often mobilised in order to push particular political agendas or strategies, while at the same time denying the political component of these through an invocation of ethics.[4] Fagan and Zehfuss both call for a reconsideration of our separation between ethics and politics in order to envision decisions as 'ethico-political' challenges.

What is at stake here is the way ethics is *invoked* by political actors in an increasing array of policy domains in order to make certain policies possible, while at the same time taming politics. This is particularly problematic in the field of scientific and technological innovation,

---

[2] Zehfuss 2018.   [3] Zehfuss 2018, p. 12.   [4] Fagan 2013.

because there often is no pre-existing societal consensus on what kind of normative framework should govern new questions which emerge. By shifting ethics into the realm of expertise, policymakers can obfuscate the political nature of such decisions and avoid democratic discussions that may stall scientific innovation.

Beyond Europe

These observations, gathered through in-depth case study research across three policy domains in the EU context, have a broader reach. The genealogy of expertise presented in Chapter 3 of the book reveals that in the United States, France and Germany, ethics committees have helped make scientific and technological innovation, as well as the commercialisation of associated technological applications, possible. Preliminary research on the contemporary role of bioethics experts in the United States confirms similar dynamics. Social scientists have well documented the politicisation of the national bioethics commission in the United States. Existing accounts essentially focus on the case of hESC research.[5] The Clinton, Bush and Obama administrations have all taken distinct policies regarding federal funding for hESC, and ethics experts have each time been mobilised in an attempt to facilitate the executive's agenda. To consider a less widely known example of ethics experts' mobilisation, let's pause on the case of synthetic biology, which was far less publicised and does not seem to be an obvious candidate for politicisation. It was further to a request from President Obama in May 2010 that the Presidential Commission for the Study of Bioethical Issues (PCSBI)[6] started to reflect on the ethics of synthetic biology. Barack Obama's request followed the announcement that Dr John Craig Venter, a superstar geneticist in the United States, had gone a step further in his quest to create synthetic life by inserting a laboratory-made genome into a bacterial cell, hence creating an organism 'not found in nature'.[7] Friends of the Earth and other NGOs immediately voiced their concerns, denouncing synthetic biology as dangerous and stating that 'Mr. Venter should stop all further research until sufficient regulations are in place'.[8] Invoking the precautionary principle, NGOs

---

[5] See, for instance, Gottweiss 2005; Briggle 2009; Leinhos 2005.
[6] The PCSBI, set up by Barack Obama at the beginning of his mandate, replaced the President's Council on Bioethics formerly appointed by George W. Bush.
[7] Wade 2010.   [8] Friends of the Earth 2010.

swiftly called for 'a moratorium on the release and commercial use of synthetic organisms until a thorough study of all the environmental and socio-economic impacts of this emerging technology has taken place'.[9] In October 2010, the United Nations Convention on Biological Diversity also voted a declaration that recognised this technology's potential environmental threat, particularly in its application to the production of biofuels.

Synthetic biology has many potential applications, some of them related to biofuels – the development of which Obama wanted to promote. In his 2011 State of the Union address, Barack Obama argued that the United States needed more research to develop biofuels in order to cut the country's oil dependency.[10] The NGO protests that had started to emerge represented a threat to the executive's agenda and Obama needed to contain conflict. In his request to the PCSBI, Barack Obama asked ethics experts for suggestions to ensure that the United States 'reaps the benefits of the developing field [of synthetic biology] within appropriate ethical boundaries', in a clear attempt to delineate the contours of experts' discussions.[11] In its final report, the PCSBI called for 'prudent vigilance' in the field of synthetic biology but did not suggest any regulatory constraints.[12] Dr Amy Gutmann, then chair of the expert group, commented, 'We chose a middle course to maximise public benefits while also safeguarding against risks'.[13] Here too, as in the case of EU policies on data protection and hESC research examined in this book, ethics experts provided the executive with a conciliating rhetoric, designed to tame conflict. Friends of the Earth and another fifty-seven NGOs addressed a letter to Amy Gutmann on the day the group published its report. They attacked the report, in particular the 'prudent vigilance' concept which they claimed had no legal or policy precedents.[14] By contrast, industry trade groups, scientific groups and the White House Office of Science and Technology policy were satisfied with the PCSBI recommendations.

Commentators saw the experts' report as a 'green light' for synthetic biology.[15] The PCSBI recommendations were indeed broadly in line

---

[9] Friends of the Earth et al. 2010.
[10] See the 2011 State of the Union speech from Barack Obama: White House Office of the Press Secretary 2011.
[11] See his letter: Obama 2010.
[12] Presidential Commission for the Study of Bioethical Issues 2010.
[13] Gutmann 2011. [14] Darnovsky 2010. [15] Pollack 2010.

with the President's position on the issue. While the PCSBI experts identified potential risks, in their view these did not justify major obstructions but 'a well-coordinated system of federal oversight'.[16] Environmental activists have continued to call for a moratorium, denouncing some companies for already using synthetic biology ingredients without alerting consumers.[17] Despite the NGO protests, the US government has not set any restrictions on synthetic biology research. By involving ethics experts in policy, Obama was able to make the case that synthetic biology research was conducted within ethical boundaries – as defined by experts. The executive's agenda was made less contestable and conflict did not expand beyond a narrow circle of NGOs.

This brief sketch of the synthetic biology case in the United States brings to light that ethics experts were mobilised in a situation where the executive had a clear agenda and aimed to contain conflict on the issue of synthetic biology. Green activists had voiced their concerns and Obama needed 'ethics' in order to push his agenda forward. The PCSBI experts also provided him with a seemingly reconciling concept – that of 'prudent diligence' – which the President could then smartly mobilise in order to show a certain awareness of the risks related to synthetic biology while not preventing research (and commercialisation) in the field. Here, too, the mobilisation of ethics depoliticised the issue at stake and made scientific innovation possible.

Although the democratic path is available in domestic contexts, policymakers might fear this route when a broad inclusion of stakeholders in the policy process is unlikely to yield consensus or even political compromise.

Policymakers mandate experts in a wide array of policy domains. Experts are called into policy to evaluate risks related to new medicines, new financial products, recidivist criminal behaviour or terrorism. Existing research has evidenced the limited ability of such experts to grasp signals of upcoming failures or disasters, problems of conflicts of interests, or phenomena of regulatory capture.[18] Groups of experts in ethics have, for their part, been portrayed as more deliberative and pluralistic forums and, as such, as a remedy to some of these ills. The revealing of the political nature of bioethical expertise, as well as the

---

[16] Presidential Commission for the Study of Bioethical Issues 2010.
[17] Strom 2014. [18] Demortain 2017.

continuing enmeshment of ethics experts with those who do policy, alerts us to their limited ability to play such roles. A remedy to this would be to develop mechanisms to facilitate the substantive participation of citizens most directly affected by decisions in these domains, either at the domestic or at the supranational level: for example consumers, patients, factory workers or engineers who make new products the safety of which is uncertain. Such participation would make for more open debates, as well as policy solutions that balance out a broader diversity of preferences.

Expertise and Politics in Global Governance

This book provides us with fresh insights concerning the fabric of expertise in global governance. In revealing the enmeshment between the production of expertise and politics, it feeds into an emerging research agenda in IR, sociology and also anthropology, which has revealed that global agendas, policies and programmes are fabricated by or within exclusive transnational fields,[19] communities,[20] networks[21] and 'clubs',[22] which gather actors from public institutions, the private sector, academia or NGOs, and which form the locus where knowledge and policy agendas are fabricated. Such scholarship has shed light on the need to focus on *iterations* between these actors in order to understand how certain ways of knowing and seeing emerge and become dominant.

All these contributions, while having their own specificities, point to the way global governance, although performed by actors coming from different spheres, is highly exclusive. Only those actors who either already adhere to a certain discourse, have been socialised together, share similar expertise, or have access to specific resources can become members of such communities, networks or clubs.[23] While some accounts see actors' adherence to a similar discourse as a precondition for participation, others conceive transnational networks or communities as the locus where discourses are articulated. Stone, for instance, sheds light on the way public servants, experts and international bureaucrats work together in transnational policy communities, where 'specific

---

[19] Sending 2015.   [20] Stone 2017; Djelic and Quack 2010.
[21] Biersteker 2014.   [22] Tsingou 2015.
[23] Dobner 2007; Schneiker and Joachim 2018; Seabrooke and Tsingou 2009; Seabrooke and Henriksen 2017.

policy ideas or a slowly built scientific consensus become an organising logic or coordinative policy paradigm'.[24] It is in these communities, she argues, that experts and professionals create knowledge and articulate narratives which inform global governance. Tsingou, in her analysis of the global governance of finance, shows how a very exclusive group of high-profile individuals both from the public and the private sphere, who share a common goal, come to decide on the way in which finance should be governed on a global scale. Whether ideas are seen as a precondition for participation in such groups or as a result of group interaction once they are in place, such accounts emphasise the way networks, communities and clubs act as arenas where dominant narratives are fabricated, stabilised or diffused. They also point to the constant iterations between a diverse set of actors coming from the public and private spheres, thus revealing the limitations of accounts that focus on the influence of a specific type of actors over policy.

IR scholars have also pointed to the role of specific individuals who are blurring roles across sectors and/or organisations. These individuals – the 'boundary spanners' – 'enjoy familiarity'[25] in different organisations and settings and can transfer their experience and expertise across these different spaces.[26] Holzscheiter, for instance, explains that these individuals are able to build bridges across different spheres, facilitating both coordination and problem definition.[27] The way they travel across different spheres, either simultaneously or successively, contributes to the fabric of dominant and uncontested discourses in global governance.[28] Seabrooke and Tsingou, who examine how coalitions within and amongst professional ecologies fight over the definition of problems, point to the centrality of the 'revolving door' phenomenon through which individuals are detached from their formal affiliations and move across spheres.[29] Those actors who are able to link ideas and skills across ecologies typically succeed in capturing policy debates and shaping policy. This perspective focuses on the role of *specific individuals* who act across organisations and sectors and contribute to harmonising agendas in these spaces either through strategic action or the diffusion of ideas.

---

[24] Stone 2017, p. 100.   [25] Boari and Riboldazzi 2014.
[26] Crouch and Farrel 2004.   [27] Holzscheiter 2017.
[28] See also Demortain 2008 on this phenomenon.
[29] Seabrooke and Tsingou 2009.

Such accounts focus on the function either of the community, club or network itself in articulating such discourses, or on the role of individuals who work and act across different arenas and promote certain ideas. In some accounts it is the belonging of these actors to the community that is interpreted as resulting in the production or stabilisation of common assumptions and ways of tackling problems. Morgan, for instance, emphasises the role of interactions within transnational communities that lead to shared understandings.[30] In others, the focus is on specific persons, typically high-profile professionals who succeed through their multiple cross-sectorial appointments in diffusing certain discourses or ideas.

While innovative and illuminating, these accounts do not give a complete picture of the mechanisms that make these global narratives so stable. Interactions within networks or communities, as well as the circulation of specific individuals, certainly play out in the production or stabilisation of common assumptions and ideas. But why do such narratives remain stable even when they are contested? And what is the role of power and resources within and around such networks and how do these play out in the stabilisation of such narratives? Why do experts who participate in or advise such communities essentially adhere to these narratives? By focusing on logics of iteration between experts, policymakers and private actors, the book identifies specific mechanisms through which certain narratives become incontestable and experts come to share these.

The book reveals that three logics of iteration between experts, policymakers and private actors (orchestration, ideational alignment and calibration) act as mechanisms of stabilisation. I argue, first, that *ideational alignment* takes place through the participation of experts and policymakers in crossing points – those spaces where policymakers and scientists meet, talk and deliberate – which induces the production of ways of approaching policy problems that become common to experts and policymakers alike. These crossing points can be work meetings, conferences, fairs, consultative forums, reflection forums or roundtables. In these arenas, experts and all other actors involved in the governance of a given domain develop common ways of knowing and approaching policy problems. The logic of ideational alignment accounts for the way actors' positions are *brought into line* through

[30] Morgan 2001.

repeated meetings in tangible spaces, rather than just being there because the actors belong to a transnational community or network. The point is not to deny that actors may have some degree of autonomy and agency when they formulate their views on specific policy problems. But common assumptions and ideas constructed or stabilised in these crossing points result in certain ways of approaching problems becoming uncontested, thus compromising the viability of certain alternatives.

In addition to ideational alignment, *orchestration* may also be at play. Some actors within the policy community may orchestrate the way other participants – including experts – think about the issue at stake. Power and resources can determine which actors are in a position to shape the contours of policy debates in a given policy domain. Hierarchies may exist within communities or networks, potentially leading to phenomena of capture by certain actors. In the case of bioethics, policymakers have been able to shape the work of bioethics experts. This has also happened in other domains, such as security.[31] Private actors may also dominate the governance of a given domain and be able to orchestrate discussions in a way which is advantageous to their preferences. Tsingou points to how 'economic ideas about what constitutes appropriate financial regulation have mirrored private sector practices and exhibited a strong bias against political meddling' in the case of global finance.[32] Demortain reveals how private actors (the pharmaceutical industry) has been able to capture the way pharmaceuticals are regulated and evaluated at the global level.[33] Orchestration can be direct when policymakers ask experts specific questions, thus delineating what they can reflect upon. It can be more diffuse when private actors make the case that they have unique specialised expertise or know-how and use such claims to legitimise self-regulation of hybrid forms of governance. It can even be opaque when private actors, for instance, work with certain NGOs or professional organisations in order to further their preferences through intermediary actors.[34] The logic of orchestration allows us to decipher when agency is at work and when power dynamics give more leverage to certain participants.

Finally, a third logic contributes to the stability of certain narratives and their associated forms of knowledge in policy domains. Some

[31] Niederberger 2020. [32] Tsingou 2015, p. 225. [33] Demortain 2015.
[34] Littoz-Monnet 2020.

governance actors, whether experts, activists, policymakers or even private actors, may intentionally calibrate their claims, either because they think it is appropriate or because they do not want to be excluded from the circle of actors that has a say in the governance of their domain. Actors of a policy community may not always think the same way just because they interact with other actors of the community on a regular basis. But *calibration* refers to the way certain positions are made more acceptable to all or are brought into line with dominant narratives. In such circumstances agency is used to adjust to, rather than oppose, dominant discourses. Actors may calibrate their position and claims, for instance, when they fear being excluded. Actors may indeed fear not being invited any longer to participate in specific crossing points, such as conferences or work meetings. Orchestration may also result from an internalisation of the sense that policy needs to proceed and that too much resistance is counterproductive, or from a general understanding that problems should be discussed in a technical 'expert' fashion, leading to forms of discussions that never question the overarching assumptions upon which certain narratives and their associated policies are based.

The co-legitimation of knowledge and politics is the product of these specific iteration mechanisms between experts, policymakers and, often, private actors, which are not only analytically distinguishable but also (often) empirically observable. At the meso-level of the governance of a policy domain, when actors come to decide about which problems should be addressed and how, explicit or sometimes more tacit conflicts abound. Dominant discourses or ways of seeing things, as well as the knowledge these rely on, are often contested. Yet, and despite such controversies, dominant narratives and their associated types of expertise tend to be stable, whether in health, finance, security or environment, even when conflicts pepper the shaping of global agendas and programmes. Expertise, the knowledge that is authoritative in a given domain, and which both informs and is legitimised by politics, despite being contested and perhaps 'disenchanted' or provisional, remains resilient.[35] Although contestation does take place, which experts and what forms of knowledge are seen as authoritative remains stable despite critique.

---

[35] Best 2014; Kennedy 2016; Leander and Waever 2018.

Annex European Group of Ethics Experts 1991–2020

Year	Name	Nationality	Area of Specialisation
1991–1997	Noëlle Lenoir	France	Law
	Margareta Mikkelsen	Denmark	Genetics
	Anne McLaren	United Kingdom	Biology
	Luis Archer	Portugal	Genetics
	Gilbert Hottois	Belgium	Philosophy
	Dietmar Mieth	Germany	Philosophy and theology
	Octavi Quintana-Trias	Spain	Medicine
	Stefano Rodota	Italy	Law
	Egbert Schroten	Netherlands	Philosophy and theology
1998–2000	Noëlle Lenoir	France	Law
	Octavi Quintana-Trias	Spain	Medicine
	Paula Martinho da Silva	Portugal	Law
	Anne McLaren	United Kingdom	Genetics
	Marja Sorsa	Finland	Biology
	Ina Wagner	Austria	Multidisciplinary systems designs and computer-supported cooperative work
	Göran Hermerén	Sweden	Philosophy
	Gilbert Hottois	Belgium	Philosophy
	Dietmar Mieth	Germany	Philosophy and theology
	Stefano Rodota	Italy	Law
	Egbert Schroten	Netherlands	Philosophy and theology
	Peter Whittaker	Ireland	Biology

(*cont.*)

Year	Name	Nationality	Area of Specialisation
2000–2005	Göran Hermerén	Sweden	Philosophy
	Linda Nielsen	Denmark	Law
	Nikos C. Alivizatos	Greece	Law
	Inez de Beaufort	Netherlands	Medical ethics
	Rafael Capurro	Germany	Information management and information ethics
	Yvon Englert	Belgium	Medical ethics and deontology
	Catherine Labrusse-Riou	France	Law
	Anne McLaren	United Kingdom	Genetics
	Pere Puigdomènech Rosell	Spain	Biology and genomics
	Stefano Rodota	Italy	Law
	Günter Virt	Austria	Theology
	Peter Whittaker	Ireland	Biology
2005–2010	Göran Hermerén	Sweden	Philosophy
	Paula Martinho da Silva	Portugal	Law
	Emmanuel Agius	Malta	Moral philosophy and moral theology
	Diána Bánáti	Hungary	Food safety
	Francesco donato Busnelli	Italy	Law
	Anne Cambon-Thomsen	France	Genetics and public health
	Rafael Capurro	Germany	Information management and information ethics
	Inez de Beaufort	Netherlands	Medical ethics
	Jozef Glasa	Slovak Republic	Medicine
	Hille Haker	Germany	Catholic moral theology

Annex

(*cont.*)

Year	Name	Nationality	Area of Specialisation
	Julian Kinderlerer	United Kingdom/ South Africa	Law
	Krzysztof Marczewski	Poland	Medicine
	Linda Nielsen	Denmark	Law
	Pere Puigdomènech Rosell	Spain	Biology and genomics
	Günter Virt	Austria	Theology
2011–2016	Emmanuel Agius	Malta	Moral philosophy and moral theology
	Inez de Beaufort	Netherlands	Medical ethics
	Peter Dabrock	Germany	Systematic theology
	Andrzej Gorski	Poland	Medicine
	Hille Haker	Germany	Catholic moral theology
	Ritva Halila	Finland	Medical ethics
	Julian Kinderlerer	United Kingdom/ South Africa	Law
	Paula Martinho da Silva	Portugal	Law
	Linda Nielsen	Denmark	Law
	Herman Nys	Belgium	Medicine law
	Siobhan O'Sullivan	Ireland	Bioethics
	Laura Palazzani	Italy	Law
	Pere Puigdomènech Rosell	Spain	Biology and genomics
	Marie-Jo Thiel	France	Bioethics
	Günter Virt	Austria	Theology
2017–2019	Emmanuel Agius	Malta	Moral philosophy and moral theology
	Anne Cambon-Thomsen	France	Genetics and public health
	Ana Sofia Carvalho	Portugal	Bioethics
	Eugenijus Gefenas	Lithuania	Medical ethics

(*cont.*)

Year	Name	Nationality	Area of Specialisation
	Julian Kinderlerer	United Kingdom/ South Africa	Law
	Andreas Kurtz	Germany	Biology
	Jonathan Montgomery	United Kingdom	Health care law
	Herman Nys	Belgium	Medicine law
	Siobhan O'Sullivan	Ireland	Bioethics
	Laura Palazzani	Italy	Law
	Barbara Prainsack	United Kingdom	Bioethics
	Carlos Maria Romeo Casabona	Spain	Law
	Nils-Eric Sahlin	Sweden	Medical ethics
	Marcel Jeroen Van den Hoven	Netherlands	Ethics and technology
	Christiane Woopen	Germany	Ethics and medicine

Bibliography

Abbott, Andrew (1988). *The System of Professions: An Essay on the Division of Expert Labor*, Chicago: University of Chicago Press.

Abélès, Marc and Irène Bellier (1996). Le Commission européenne du compromis culturel à la culture du compromis. *Revue Française de Science Politique*, 46(3), 431–56.

Abels, Gabriele and Alsons Bora (2004). *Demokratische Technikbewertung*, Bielefeld: Transcript Verlag.

Abrahamson, Eric (1991). Managerial fads and fashions: The diffusion and rejection of innovations. *Academy of Management Review*, 16(3), 586–612.

Action Group on Erosion, Technology and Concentration (ETC Group) (2003). *The Big Down: Atomtech – Technologies Converging at the Nanoscale*. www.etcgroup.org/sites/www.etcgroup.org/files/thebigdown.pdf

Ad Hoc Committee of the Harvard Medical School to Examine the Definition of Brain Death (1968). A definition of reversible coma. *JAMA* 205(6), 337–40.

Ahlstrom, Dick (2003, 5 November). Row over stem cell research funding, *Irish Times*.

Anderson, William F. (1971). Genetic Therapy. In Michael P. Hamilton, ed., *The New Genetics and the Future of Man*, Grand Rapids, MI: William B. Eerdmans, pp. 15–63.

Anon. (1977). Complaints by patients. *Lancet*, 310, 1238.

Arnall, Alexander H. (2003). *Future Technologies, Today's Choices: Nanotechnology, Artificial Intelligence, and Robotics; A Technical, Political, and Institutional Map of Emerging Technologies Technologies: A Report for the Greenpeace Environmental Trust*, London: Department of Environmental Science and Technology Environmental Policy and Management Group, Faculty of Life Sciences, Imperial College London, University of London.

Bachrach, Peter and Morton S. Baratz (1962). Two faces of power. *American Political Science Review*, 56(4), 947–52.

Barnett, Michael N. and Martha Finnemore (2004). *Rules for the World: International Organizations in Global Politics*, Ithaca, NY: Cornell University Press.

Barroso, José Manuel (2011, 21 March). Letter to Julian Kinderlerer, president of the European Group on Ethics on the ethical implications of ICT technologies.
Bauman, Zygmunt (2005). *Liquid Life*, Cambridge: Polity Press.
Baumgartner, Frank R., Suzanna De Boef and Amber Boydstun (2008). *The Decline of the Death Penalty and the Discovery of Innocence*, New York: Cambridge University Press.
Beauchamp, Tom L. and James F. Childress (2019). *Principles of Biomedical Ethics*, 8th ed., New York and Oxford: Oxford University Press.
Beecher, Henry (1966). Ethics in clinical research. *New England Journal of Medicine*, 274(24), 1354–60.
Bell, Daniel (1960). *The End of Ideology: On the Exhaustion of Political Ideas in the Fifties*, Glencoe, IL: Free Press.
Benveniste, Guy (1972). *The Politics of Expertise*, Berkeley: Glendessary Press.
Berg, Paul (2008). Meetings that changed the world: Asilomar 1975: DNA modification secured. *Nature*, 455(7211), 290–1.
Berndtsson, Johakim (2012). Security professionals for hire: Exploring the many faces of private security expertise. *Millennium Journal of International Studies* 40(2), 300–17.
Best, Jaqueline (2014). *Governing Failure: Provisional Expertise and the Transformation of Global Development Finance*, Cambridge: Cambridge University Press.
Biersteker, Thomas (2014). Participating in Transnational Policy Networks: Targeted Sanctions. In Mariano E. Bertucci and Abraham F. Lowenthal, eds., *Scholars, Policymakers and International Affairs: Finding Common Cause*, Baltimore and London: Johns Hopkins University Press. pp. 137–54.
Birkland, T. A. (1998). Focusing events, mobilization, and agenda setting. *Journal of Public Policy* 18(1), 53–74.
Boari, Cristina and Federico Riboldazzi (2014). How knowledge brokers emerge and evolve: The role of actors' behaviour. *Research Policy*, 43(4), 683–95.
Boschk, Xavier (2005, 4 November). Concerns over new EU ethics panel. The Scientist. www.the-scientist.com/?articles.view/articleNo/23494/title/Concerns-over-new-EU-ethics-panel
Bosk, Charles L. (1999). Professional ethicist available: Logical, secular, friendly. *Daedelus*, 128(4), 47–68.
Boswell, Christina (2009). *The Political Uses of Expert Knowledge: Immigration Policy and Social Research*, Cambridge and New York: Cambridge University Press.
Braun, Kathrin (2005). Not just for experts: The public debate about reprogenetics in Germany. *Hastings Center Report*, 35(3), 42–9.

Braun, Kathrin, Svea Luise Herrmann, Alfred Moore and Sabine Könninger (2010). Science governance and the politics of proper talk: Governmental bioethics as a new technology of reflexive government. *Economy and Society*, 39(4), 510–33.
Braun, Kathrin and Cordula Kropp (2010). Beyond speaking truth? Institutional responses to uncertainty in scientific governance. *Science, Technology and Human Values*, 35(6), 771–82.
Briggle, Adam (2009). The Kass Council and the politicization of ethics advice. *Social Studies of Science* 39(2), 309–26.
Brown, Eric (2004). The dilemmas of German bioethics. *New Atlantis*, 5, 37–53.
Bundesministerium für Gesundheit (2000). *Science symposium of the German Health Ministry in collaboration with the Robert Koch Institute, held May 24–6, 2000, in Berlin*. Baden-Baden: Nomos.
Bureau of European Policy Advisers (BEPA) (2014) Activities 2011–2016. https://ec.europa.eu/archives/bepa/european-group-ethics/welcome/activities/index_en.htm
Callahan, Daniel (1973). Bioethics as a discipline. *Hastings Center Studies*, 1 (1), 66–73.
Callahan, Daniel (1990). Religion and the secularization of bioethics. *Hastings Center Report*, 20(4), 2–4.
Callon, Michel, Pierre Lascoumes and Yannick Barthe (2009). *Acting in an Uncertain World: An Essay on Technical Democracy*, Cambridge, MA: MIT Press.
Caplan, Nathan (1979). The two-communities theory and knowledge utilization. *American Behavioral Scientist*, 22(3), 459–70.
Clark, Matt (1975, 30 November). A right to die? *Newsweek*.
Clark, Nick and Robert Verkaik (2009, 14 April). Internet privacy: Britain in the dock. 'Big Brother' state comes under fire as European Commission launches inquiry into secret surveillance of web users. *The Independent*.
Commission of the Bishops' Conferences of the European Community (COMECE) (2005, 6 April). Research in the light of human dignity [Press release]. www.comece.eu/site/en/ourwork/pressreleases/2005/article/7578.html
'Competitive council: Political deal secured on 7th framework research programme' (2006, 25 July). *European Report*.
CORDIS (Community Research and Development Information Service) (2003). Nanotechnology: Opportunity or threat? https://cordis.europa.eu/news/rcn/20401_en.html
CORDIS (Community Research and Development Information Service) (2005). EURAB urges scientific community to lobby ministers on FP7

budget. https://cordis.europa.eu/article/id/23927-eurab-urges-scientific-community-to-lobby-ministers-on-fp7-budget

CORDIS (Community Research and Development Information Service) (2008). Commission adopts code of conduct for responsible nano research. http://cordis.europa.eu/news/rcn/29114_en.html

CORDIS (Community Research and Development Information Service) (2012). Europe plans ahead on nanobiotechnology. http://cordis.europa.eu/result/rcn/88336_en.html

Council of the European Union (2003). 2550th Council meeting: Competitiveness – internal market, industry and research. C/03/355. https://ec.europa.eu/commission/presscorner/detail/en/PRES_03_355

Council of the European Union (2006). Competitiveness (internal market, industry and research) [Press release: 2747th council meeting, Brussels, 24 July]. www.consilium.europa.eu/ueDocs/cms_Data/docs/pressData/en/intm/90654.pdf

Crouch, Colin and Henry Farrell (2004). Breaking the path of institutional development? Alternatives to the new determinism. *Rationality and Society*, 16(1), 5–43.

Darnovsky, Marcy (2010, 16 December). Bioethics commission on synthetic biology: 'Prudent vigilance' or green light?, *Biopolitical Times*.

Daviter, Falk (2009). Schattschneider in Brussels: How policy conflict reshaped the biotechnology agenda in the European Union. *West European Politics*, 32(6), 1118–39.

Daviter, Falk (2015). The political use of knowledge in the policy process. *Policy Sciences*, 48(4), 491–505.

De Vlieger, Pieterjan and Irina Tanasescu (2012). Changing forms of interactions between the European Commission and interest groups: The case of religious lobbying. *Journal of European Integration*, 34(5), 447–63.

Demortain, David (2008). Standardising through concepts: The power of scientific experts in international standard-setting. *Science and Public Policy*, 35(6), 391–402.

Demortain, David (2015). The tools of globalization: Ways of regulating and the structure of the international regime for pharmaceuticals. *Review of International Political Economy*, 22(6), 1249–75.

Demortain, David (2017). Expertise, regulatory science and the evaluation of technology and risk: Introduction to special issue. *Minerva*, 55(2), 139–59.

Department of Health (United Kingdom) (2000). Stem cell research: Medical progress with responsibility: A report from the Chief Medical Officer's expert group reviewing the potential of developments in stem cell research and cell nuclear replacement to benefit human health. *Cloning* 2(2), 91–6.

Bibliography

Devos, Yann, Dirk Reheul, Danny de Waele and Linda van Speybroeck (2006). The interplay between societal concerns and the regulatory frame on GM crops in the European Union. *Environmental Biosafety Research*, 5(3), 127–49.

Digital Europe (2013, 28 August). DigitalEurope Comments on the Risk-Based Approach. https://teknologiateollisuus.fi/sites/default/files/file_at tachments/elinkeinopolitiikka_digitalisaatio_tietosuoja_digitaleurope_r isk_based_approach.pdf

Digital Europe (2015). Open Statement Ahead of Expected Final Trilogue on General Data Protection Regulation, 14 December 2015. www.digitaleurope .org/resources/open-statement-ahead-of-expected-final-trilogue-on-general-d ata-protection-regulation

Djelic, Marie-Laure and Sigrid Quack (eds.) (2010). *Transnational Communities: Shaping Global Economic Governance*, Cambridge: Cambridge University Press.

Dobner, Petra (2007). Did the state fail? Zur Transnationalisierung und Privatisierung der öffentlichen Daseinsfürsorge: Die Reform der globalen Trinkwasserpolitik. In Klaus Dieter Wolf, ed., *Staat und Gesellschaft – fähig zur Reform? 23. wissenschaftlicher Kongress der Deutschen Vereinigung für Politikwissenschaft*. Nomos: Baden-Baden, pp. 247–61.

Edwards, Robert G. and David J. Sharpe (1971). Social values and research in human embryology. *Nature*, 231(5298), 87–91.

Elvins, Martin (2003). *Anti-Drugs Policies of the European Union: Transnational Decision-Making and the Politics of Expertise*, New York: Palgrave MacMillan.

Engeli, Isabelle and Frederic Varone (2011). Governing morality issues through procedural policies. *Swiss Political Science Review*, 17(3), 239–58.

'EU votes on stem cells fail to solve problem' (2003, 28 November). *Times Higher Education*.

'EU politicians say funding plan focuses too much on biotech, genomics' (2001, 13 November). *Reuters*.

EURACTIV (2007). NGOS urge precautionary principle in use of nanomaterials. www.euractiv.com/section/climate-environment/news/ng os-urge-precautionary-principle-in-use-of-nanomaterials

European Chemicals Agency (ECHA) (n.d.). Nanomaterials. http://echa .europa.eu/web/guest/regulations/nanomaterials

European Commission (2001a). Proposal for Council Decision Concerning the Specific Programmes Implementing the Framework Programme 2002–2006 of the European Community for Research, Technological Development and Demonstration Activities, COM(2001) 279 final.

European Commission (2001b, 12 September). EU supports and coordinates stem cell research [Press release]. https://ec.europa.eu/research/press/2001/pr1409en.html

European Commission (2003a). Commission Staff Working Paper: Report on Human Embryonic Stem Cell Research, COM(2003) 390 final.

European Commission (2003b, 9 July). European Commission proposes strict ethical guidelines on EU funding of human embryonic stem cell research [Press release]. http://europa.eu/rapid/press-release_IP-03-969_en.htm?locale=en

European Commission (2004a). Towards a European Strategy for Nanotechnology, COM(2004) 338.

European Commission (2004b). Nanotechnologies: A Preliminary Risk Analysis on the Basis of a Workshop Organized in Brussels on 1–2 March 2004 by the Health and Consumer Protection Directorate General of the European Commission. https://ec.europa.eu/health/ph_risk/documents/ev_20040301_en.pdf

European Commission (2005a). Proposal for a Council Decision Concerning the Specific Programme 'Cooperation' Implementing the 7th Framework Programme of the European Community for Research, Technological Development and Demonstration Activities, COM(2005) 440 final.

European Commission (2005b). Nanosciences and Nanotechnologies: An Action Plan for Europe 2005–2009, COM (2005) 243 final.

European Commission (2008a). Communication from the Commission to the European Parliament, the Council and the European Economic and Social Committee – Regulatory Aspects of Nanomaterials, COM/2008/0366 final.

European Commission (2008b). Recommendation of 7 February 2008 on a Code of Conduct for Responsible Nanosciences and Nanotechnologies Research, C(2008) 424.

European Commission (2010a). Communication from the Commission EUROPE 2020: A Strategy for Smart, Sustainable and Inclusive Growth, COM(2010) 2020.

European Commission (2010b). Communication from the Commission: A Digital Agenda for Europe, COM (2010) 245 final/2.

European Commission (2010c). Communication from the Commission: A Comprehensive Approach on Personal Data Protection in the European Union, COM(2010) 609.

European Commission (2014). Communication from the Commission: Towards a Thriving Data-driven Economy, COM (2014) 442 final.

European Commission Research Directorate General (2001). Stem Cell Research at European Level.

European Consumer Voice in Standardisation (ANEC) and European Consumers' Organisation (BEUC) (2009). Nanotechnology: Small Is Beautiful but Is It Safe? www.anec.eu/attachments/ANEC-PT-2009-Nano-002final.pdf

European Council (2003). Conclusions of Competitiveness Council of 3 December 2003, 2550th Council Meeting, C/03/355.

European Council (2006). Conclusions of Competitiveness Council of 24 July 2006, 10633/1/06/REV1.

European Data Protection Supervisor (2015). Opinion 7: Meeting the Challenges of Big Data. A Call for Transparency, User Control, Data Protection by Design and Accountability, Opinion 7.

European Digital Rights (EDRi) (2012). Initial Comments on the Proposal for a Data Protection Regulation, 27 January 2012. https://edri.org/commentsdpr

European Group on Ethics in Science and New Technologies (EGE) (2000). Opinion 15: Ethical Aspects of Human Stem Cell Research and Use.

European Group on Ethics in Science and New Technologies (EGE) (2006). The Ethical Aspects of Nanomedicine. Proceedings of the Roundtable Debate, Brussels, 21 March. https://ec.europa.eu/archives/european_group_ethics/archive/2005_2010/activities/docs/roundt_nano_21march2006_final_en.pdf

European Group on Ethics in Science and New Technologies (EGE) (2007a). Opinion 22: Recommendations on the Ethical Review of hESC FP7 Research Projects.

European Group on Ethics in Science and New Technologies (EGE) (2007b). Opinion 21: Opinion on Ethical Aspects of Nanomedicine.

European Group on Ethics in Science and New Technologies (EGE) (2012). Opinion 26: Ethics of Information and Communication Technologies.

European Group on Ethics in Science and New Technologies (EGE) (2014). Opinion 28: Ethics of Security and Surveillance Technologies.

European Parliament (2000). Resolution on Human Cloning, PE T5-0375/2000.

European Parliament (2005). Resolution on the Trade in Human Egg Cells, P6 TA(2005) 0074 10.

European Parliament (2009). Motion for a Resolution on Regulatory Aspects of Nanomaterials, 2008/2208(INI).

European Parliament (2012). Draft Report on the Protection of Individuals with Regard to the Processing of Personal Data by Competent Authorities for the Purposes of Prevention, Investigation, Detection or Prosecution of Criminal Offences or the Execution of Criminal Penalties, and the Free Movement of such Data, 2012/0010 (COD).

European Parliament (2013). Report on the Proposal for a Regulation on the Protection of Individuals with regard to the Processing of Personal Data and on the Free Movement of Such Data (General Data Protection Regulation), A7–0402/2013.

European Parliament and Council (2002). Decision No 1513/2002/EC of the European Parliament and of the Council of 27 June 2002 concerning the sixth framework programme of the European Community for research, technological development and demonstration activities, contributing to the creation of the European Research Area and to innovation (2002 to 2006). *Official Journal of the European Communities* L 232.

European Parliament and Council (2006). Regulation of 18 December 2006 Concerning the Registration, Evaluation, Authorisation and Restriction of Chemicals (REACH), Establishing a European Chemicals Agency, Amending Directive 1999/45/EC and Repealing Council Regulation (EEC) No 793/93 and Commission Regulation (EC) No 1488/94 as Well as Council Directive 76/769/EEC and Commission Directives 91/155/EEC, 93/67/EEC, 93/105/EC and 2000/21/EC, No. 1907/2006.

European Parliament and Council (2016a). Regulation 2016/679 of 27 April 2016 on the Protection of Natural Persons with Regard to the Processing of Personal Data and on the Free Movement of Such Data, and Repealing Directive 95/46/EC (General Data Protection Regulation), OK l119/1. https://eur-lex.europa.eu/legal-content/EN/TXT/PDF/?uri=CELEX:32016R0679&from=EN

European Parliament and Council (2016b). Directive 2016/680 of 27 April 2016 on the Protection of Natural Persons with Regard to the Processing of Personal Data by Competent Authorities for the Purposes of the Prevention, Investigation, Detection or Prosecution of Criminal Offences or the Execution of Criminal Penalties, and on the Free Movement of Such Data, and Repealing Council Framework Decision 2008/977/JHA, OJ 119/89. https://eur-lex.europa.eu/legal-content/EN/TXT/PDF/?uri=CELEX:32016L0680&from=EN

'European parties clash on stem cells' (2006, 15 June). *European Report*.

European Technology Platform for Nanomedicine (2005). Vision Paper and Basis for a Strategic Research Agenda for Nanomedcine. https://etp-nanomedicine.eu/wp-content/uploads/2018/10/COVER-2005-ETPN-Vision-paper.jpg

Evans, John H. (2002). *Playing God? Human Genetic Engineering and the Rationalization of Public Bioethical Debate*, Chicago: University of Chicago Press.

Evans, John H. (2012). *The History and Future of Bioethics: A Sociological View*, New York and Oxford: Oxford University Press.

Eyal, Gil (2013). For a sociology of expertise: The social origins of the autism epidemic, *American Journal of Sociology*, 118(4), 863–907.

Fagan, Madeleine (2013). *Ethics and Politics After Poststructuralism: Levinas, Derrida and Lancy (Taking on the Political)*, 1st ed., Edinburgh: Edinburgh University Press.

Foucault, Michel (1978). *The History of Sexuality*, New York: Pantheon Books.

Fougère, Martin and Nancy Harding (2012). On the Limits of What Can Be Said of 'Innovation': Interplay and Contrasts between Academic and Policy Discourses. In Pernilla Gripenberg, Karl-Erik Sveiby and Beata Segercrantz, eds., *Challenging the Innovation Paradigm*, New York: Routledge, pp. 15–36.

Fox, Renee C. and Judith P. Swazey (2008). *Observing Bioethics*, New York and Oxford: Oxford University Press.

Friends of the Earth (2010, 20 May). Venter takes genetic engineering to 'extreme new level'. https://foe.org/news/2010-05-venter-takes-genetic-engineering-to-extreme-new-leve

Friends of the Earth et al. (2010, 16 December). Letter to Dr Amy Gutmann, Chair, Presidential Commission for the Study of Bioethical Issues. https://1bps6437gg8c169i0y1drtgz-wpengine.netdna-ssl.com/wp-content/uploads/wpallimport/files/archive/Civil_Society_Letter_to_Presidents_Commission_on_Synthetic_Biology.pdf

Gendron, Yves, Davic J. Cooper and Barbara Townley (2007). The construction of auditing expertise in measuring government performance. *Accounting, Organizations and Society*, 32, 101–29.

'Germany calls for EU ban on stem cell research' (2006, 20 July). *The Guardian*. www.theguardian.com/science/2006/jul/20/genetics.europeanunion

Glasa, Jozef (2002). Establishment and work of ethics committees in central and eastern European countries. *Medicinska, Medical Ethics and Bioethics: Journal of the Institute of Medical Ethics & Bioethics*, 9(1–2), 9–12.

Gleenwald, Glen (2013, 6 June). 'NSA collecting phone records of millions of Verizon customers daily', *The Guardian*. www.theguardian.com/world/2013/jun/06/nsa-phone-records-verizon-court-order

Godin, Benoît (2015). Innovation: From the forbidden to a cliché, *Journal of Business Anthropology*, 4(2), 219–27.

Goldstein, Judith (1993). *Ideas, Interests and American Trade Policy*, Ithaca, NY: Cornell University Press.

Gonçalves, Maria Eduarda (2017). The EU data protection reform and the challenges of big data: Remaining uncertainties and ways forward. *Information and Communications Technology Law*, 26(2), 90–115.

Gottweiss, Herbert (2005). Stem cell policies in the United States and in Germany: Between bioethics and regulation. *Policy Studies Journal*, 30 (4), 444–69.

Gros, François, François Jacob and Pierre Royer (1979). *Sciences de la vie et sociéte´: rapport présenté à M. le Président de la République*, Paris: La Documentation Française.

Guerrier, Marc (2006). Hospital based ethics, current situation in France: Between 'espaces' and committees. *Journal of Medical Ethics*, 32(9), 503–6.

Guston, David H. (1999). Evaluating the first US consensus conference: The impact of the citizens' panel on telecommunications and the future of democracy. *Science, Technology, and Human Values* 24(4), 451–82.

Gutmann, Amy (2011). The ethics of synthetic biology: Guiding principles for emerging technologies, *Hastings Center Report*, 41(4), 17–22.

Haas, Ernst B. (1990). *When Knowledge Is Power: Three Models of Change in International Organizations*, Berkeley and Los Angeles: University of California Press.

Haas, Peter M. (1992). Introduction: Epistemic communities and international policy coordination. *International Organization*, 46(1), 1–35.

Haas, Peter and Casey Stevens (2011). Organized Science, Usable Knowledge and Multilateral Environmental Governance. In Rolf Lidskog and Göran Sundqvist, eds., *Governing the Air: The Dynamics of Science, Policy, and Citizen Interaction*, Cambridge, MA and London: MIT Press, pp. 125–62.

Haggerty, Kevin D. (2004). Ethics creep: Governing social science research in the name of ethics. *Qualitative Sociology*, 24(4), 391–414.

Harvey, John C. (2013). André Hellegers, the Kennedy Institute and the Development of Bioethics: The American-European Connection. In Jeremy R. Garrett, Fabrice Jotterand and D. Christopher Ralston, eds., *The Development of Bioethics in the United States*, New York: Springer, pp. 37–54.

Hasu, Mervi, Karl-Heinz Leitner, Urmas Varblane and Nikodemus Solitander (2012). Accelerating the Innovation Race: Do We Need Reflexive Brakes? In Pernilla Gripenberg, Karl-Erik Sveiby and Beata Segercrantz, eds., *Challenging the Innovation Paradigm*, New York: Routledge, pp. 87–112.

Heller, Jean (1972, 26 July). Syphilis victims in US study went untreated for 40 years, *New York Times*.

Hennette-Vauchez, Stéphanie (2010). *Biomedicine and EU Law: Unlikely Encounters*. European University Institute (Robert Schuman Centre for Advanced Studies), RSCAS 2010/46.

Highfield, Roger (2003, 5 June). Prince asks scientists to look into 'grey goo', *The Telegraph*.

Holzscheiter, Anna (2017). Coping with institutional fragmentation? Competition and convergence between boundary organizations in the global response to polio, *Review of Policy Research*, 34(6), 767–89.

Hoppe, Robert (2005). Rethinking the science-policy nexus: From knowledge utilisation and science technology studies to types of boundary arrangements. *Poiesis and Praxis*, 3(3), 199–215.

INRA (2017). Additif alimentaire E171: Les premiers résultats de l'exposition orale aux nanoparticules de dioxyde de titane. www.inrae.fr/actualites/additif-alimentaire-E171

Irwin, Alan, Henry Rohtstein, Steven Yearley and Elaine McCarthy (1997). Regulatory science – towards a sociological framework. *Futures*, 29(1), 17–31.

Jacobsen, John Kurt (1995). Much ado about ideas: The cognitive factor in economic policy. *World Politics* 47(1), 283–310.

Jasanoff, Sheila (1987). Contested boundaries in policy-relevant science. *Social Studies of Science*, 17(2), 195–230.

Jasanoff, Sheila (1990). *The Fifth Branch: Science Advisers as Policymakers*, Cambridge, MA: Harvard University Press.

Jasanoff, Sheila (2004). *States of Knowledge: The Co-production of Science and the Social Order*, London: Routledge.

Jasanoff, Sheila (2005). *Designs on Nature: Science and Democracy in Europe and the United States*, Princeton: Princeton University Press.

Jasanoff, Sheila and Sang-Hyun Kim (2015). *Dreamscapes of Modernity. Sociotechnical Imaginaries and the fabrication of Power*, Chicago: University of Chicago Press.

Jones, Bryan D. and Frank R. Baumgartner (2004). Representation and agenda-setting. *Policy Studies Journal*, 32(1), 1–24.

Jonsen, Albert (1998). *The Birth of Bioethics*, New York and Oxford: Oxford University Press.

Jordan, Grant A. and William A. Maloney (1997). *The Protest Business? Mobilizing Campaigning Groups* (Issues in Environmental Politics), Manchester: Manchester University Press.

Kelly, Susan E. (2003). Public bioethics and publics: Consensus, boundaries, and participation in biomedical science policy. *Science, Technology and Human Values*, 28(3), 339–64.

Kennedy, David (2016). *A World of Struggle: How Power, Law, and Expertise Shape Global Political Economy*, Princeton, NJ: Princeton University Press.

Kennedy, Ian (1980, 27 November). 'Medical ethics are not separate from but part of other ethics', *Listener*, 713–15.

Kingdon, John (2003). *Agendas, Alternatives and Public Policies*, 2nd ed., New York: Longman.

Klawiter, Maren (2008). *The Biopolitics of Breast Cancer: Changing Cultures of Disease and Activism*, Minneapolis: University of Minnesota Press.

Knill, Christoph (2013). The study of morality policy: Analytical implications from a public policy perspective. *Journal of European Public Policy*, 20(3), 309–17.

Knorr, Karin D. (1977). Policymakers' Use of Social Science Knowledge: Symbolic or Instrumental? In Carol H. Weiss, eds., *Using Social Research in Public Policy Making*, Lexington, KT: Lexington Books, pp. 165–82.

Krimsky, Sheldon (2005). From Asilomar to industrial biotechnology: Risks, reductionism and regulation. *Science as Culture*, 14(4), 309–23.

Krones, Tanja (2006). The scope of the recent bioethics debate in Germany: Kant, crisis, and no confidence in society. *Cambridge Quarterly of Healthcare Ethics*, 15(3), 273–81.

Kwak, James (2014). Cultural Capture and the Financial Crisis. In Daniel P. Carpenter and David A. Moss, eds., *Preventing Regulatory Capture: Special Interest Influence and How to Limit It*, Cambridge: Cambridge University Press, pp. 71–98.

Lane, Robert E. (1962). *Political Ideology*, New York: Free Press.

Lasswell, Harold D. and Abraham Kaplan (1950). *Power and Society: A Framework for Political Enquiry*, New Haven: Yale University Press.

Latour, Bruno (1987). *Science in Action: How to Follow Scientists and Engineers through Society*, Cambridge, MA: Harvard University Press.

Latour, Bruno (1993). *We Have Never Been Modern*. Cambridge, MA: Harvard University Press.

Leander, Anna and Ole Waever (2018). *Exclusive Expertise: Knowledge, Ignorance and Conflict Resolution in the Global South*, London: Routledge.

Leinhos, Mary (2005). The US national bioethics advisory commission as a boundary organization. *Science and Public Policy*, 32(6), 423–33.

Levine, Carol (2007). Analysing Pandora's Box: The History of Bioethics. In Lisa A. Eckenwiler and Felicia Cohn, eds., *The Ethics of Bioethics: Mapping the Moral Landscape*, Baltimore: Johns Hopkins University Press, pp. 3–23.

Levy-Abegnoli, Julie (2016, 2 May). A right to die? *Parliament Magazine*. www.theparliamentmagazine.eu/printpdf/4195

Lindblom, Charles E. and David K. Cohen (1979). *Usable Knowledge: Social Science and Social Problem Solving*, New Haven and London: Yale University Press.

Litfin, Karen (1994). *Ozone Discourses: Science and Politics in Global Environmental Cooperation: New Directions in World Politics*, New York: Columbia University Press.

Littoz-Monnet, Annabelle (2015). Ethics experts as an instrument of technocratic governance: Evidence from EU medical biotechnology policy. *Governance*, 28(3), 357–72.

Littoz-Monnet, Annabelle (2017). Expert knowledge as a strategic resource: International bureaucrats and the shaping of bioethical standards. *International Studies Quarterly*, 61(3), 584–95.

Littoz-Monnet, Annabelle (2020). The Fabric of Policy Knowledge: the Case of Global Mental Health, presented at the Swiss Political Science Association Annual Congress, February 2020, Lucerne.

Lock, Stephen (1990). Towards a national bioethics committee: Wanted: a new strategic body to deal with broad issues. *British Medical Journal*, 300(6733), 1149–50.

Lopez, José (2004). How sociology can save bioethics... maybe. *Sociology of Health and Illness*, 25(7), 875–96.

Lucas, Caroline (2003, 12 June). We must not be blinded by science: Nanotechnology will revolutionise our lives – it should be regulated, *The Guardian*.

McNamee, Joe (2016). Press Release: Vote on Data Protection and Passenger Name Record package. https://edri.org/press-release-data-protection-and-passenger-name-record-package-to-be-voted-on-tomorrow

Meyer, John W., John Boli, George M. Thomas and Francisco O. Ramirez (1997). World society and the nation-state. *American Journal of Sociology*, 103(1), 144–81.

Miller, Georgia, Lisa Archer, Erich Pica et al. (2006). *Nanomaterials, Sunscreens and Cosmetics: Small Ingredients Big Risk*. https://1bps6437gg8c169i0y1drtgz-wpengine.netdna-ssl.com/wp-content/uploads/wpalimport/files/archive/Nanomaterials_sunscreens_and_cosmetics.pdf

'MEPs sound alarm on stem cell research' (2005, 21 September). *European Report*.

Mitchell, Ronald, William C. Clark, David Cash and Nancy Dickson (2006). *Global Environmental Assessments: Information and Influence*, Cambridge: MIT Press.

Mooney, Christopher Z. and Mei Hsien Lee (2000). The influence of values on consensus and contentious morality policy: US death penalty reform, 1956–82. *Journal of Politics*, 62(1), 223–39.

Morgan, G. (2001). Transnational communities and business systems. *Global Networks*, 1(2) 113–30.

Nathoo, Ayesha (2017). The operation that took medicine into the media age. BBC News. www.bbc.com/news/health-42170023

National Commission for the Protection of Human Subjects of Biomedical and Behavioral Research (1978/1979). *Ethical Principles and Guidelines for the Protection of Human Subjects of Research* (The Belmont Report). Washington, DC: US Government Printing Office.

Nelkin, Dorothy (1975). The political impact of technical expertise. *Social Studies of Science*, 5(1), 35–54.

Nelkin, Dorothy (1995). Science Controversies: The Dynamics of Public Disputes in the United States. In Sheila Jasanoff, Gerald E. Markle, James C. Peterson and Trevor Pinch, eds., *Handbook of Science and Technology Studies*, Cambridge, MA: MIT Press, pp. 444–56.

Nerlich, Brigitte (2012, 29 June). Battle looms over European funding for embryonic stem cell research [Blog post]. http://blogs.nottingham.ac.uk/makingsciencepublic/2012/06/29/embryonic-stem-cells-eu

Niederberger, Aurel (2020). Independent experts with political mandates: 'Role distance' in the production of political knowledge. *European Journal of International Security* (forthcoming)

Nuffield Council on Bioethics (2000). *Annual Report 2000*, London: Nuffield Council on Bioethics.

O'Brien, Kevin (2009, 6 May). EU to pursue stricter law on personal data, *International Herald Tribune*.

Obama, Barack (2010, 20 May). Letter to Dr Amy Gutmann, President, and Christopher H. Browne, Distinguished Professor of Political Science. https://bioethicsarchive.georgetown.edu/pcsbi/sites/default/files/news/Letter-from-President-Obama-05.20.10.pdf

OECD (2015). *OECD Innovation Strategy 2015: An Agenda for Policy Action*. www.oecd.org/sti/OECD-Innovation-Strategy-2015-CMIN2015-7.pdf

Page, Edward (2003). The civil servant as legislator: Law making in British administration. *Public Administration* 81(4), 651–79.

'Paper sees Germany, EU, USA at odds over plan for EU-wide data privacy standards' (2012, 17 October). *BBC Monitoring Europe*.

Penissat, Etienne (2007). Entre science, administration et politique: Produire des statistiques au sein d'un ministère. *Socio-logos*, 2, 1–11.

Peters, Guy (1987). Politicians and Bureaucrats in the Politics of Policy-Making. In Jan-Erik Lane, ed., *Bureaucracy and Public Choice*, London: Sage, pp. 255–82.

Peters, Guy (1995). *The Politics of Bureaucracy*, New York: Longman.

Plomer, Aurora (2008). The European Group on Ethics: Law, politics and the limits of moral integration in Europe. *European Law Journal*, 14(6), 839–59.

Pollack, Andrew (2010, 16 December). US bioethics commission gives green light to synthetic biology. *New York Times*.

Potočnik, Janez (2007). *The European Group on Ethics in Science and New Technologies*. https://ec.europa.eu/archives/european_group_ethics/archive/2005_2010/activities/docs/speech_Potocnik12feb07_en.pdf

Presidential Commission for the Study of Bioethical Issues (2010). *New Directions: The Ethics of Synthetic Biology and Emerging Technologies*, Washington, DC.

Pressman, Jeffrey and Aaron Wildavsky (1973). *Implementation: How Great Expectations in Washington are Dashed in Oakland*. Berkeley: University of California Press.

Reding, Viviane (2010). Privacy matters – Why the EU needs new personal data protection rules. The European Data Protection and Privacy Conference, Brussels, 30 November. https://ec.europa.eu/commission/presscorner/detail/en/SPEECH_12_26

Reding, Viviane (2012). The EU Data Protection Reform 2012: Making Europe the standard setter for modern data protection rules in the digital age. Innovation Conference Digital, Life, Design, Munich, 22 January. https://ec.europa.eu/commission/presscorner/detail/en/SPEECH_10_700

Reding, Viviane (2014). Speech: A data protection compact for Europe. https://ec.europa.eu/commission/presscorner/detail/en/SPEECH_14_62

Reich, Warren T. (1994). The word 'bioethics': Its birth and the legacies of those who shaped it. *Kennedy Institute of Ethics Journal*, 4(4), 319–35.

Reinalda, Bob and Bertjan Verbeek (2003). *Autonomous Policy Making by International Organizations*, London: Routledge.

'Renewed controversy on stem-cell research' (2002, 4 September). *European Report*.

'Research: Council adopts specific programmes for FP6' (2002, 2 October). *European Report*.

Rhinard, Mark (2010). *Framing Europe: The Policy Shaping Strategies of the European Commission*, Dordrecht: Republic of Letters: Martinus Nijhoff Publishers.

Rhodes, Roderick A. W. and David Marsh (1992). New directions in the study of policy networks. *European Journal of Political Research*, 21 (1–2), 181–205.

Richardson, Jeremy J. and Grant Jordan (1979). *Governing under Pressure: The Policy Process in a Post-Parliamentary Democracy* (Government and Administration Series), Chichester: Wiley-Blackwell.

Ricoeur, Paul (1995). *Oneself as Another*, Chicago: University of Chicago Press.

Robert, Cécile (2010a). Les groupes d'experts dans le gouvernement de l'Union européenne. *Politique Européenne*, 32(3), 7–38.

Robert, Cécile (2010b). Etre Socialisé à ou par l'Europe? Dispositions Sociales et sens du jeu Institutionnel des Experts de la Commission Européenne. In Hélène Michel and Cécile Robert, eds., *La Fabrique des Européens*, Strasbourg: Presses Universitaires de Strasbourg, pp. 313–46.

Rogers, Everett (1983). *Diffusion of Innovations*. New York: Free Press.
Rothman, David J. (1982). Were Tuskegee and Willowbrook 'studies in nature'? *Hastings Center Report*, 12(2), 5–7.
Rothman, David J. (1991). *Strangers at the Bedside: A History of How Law and Bioethics Transformed Medical Decision Making*, New York: Basic Books.
Royal Society and Royal Academy of Engineers (2004). *Nanoscience and Nanotechnologies: Opportunities and Uncertainties*. www.raeng.org.uk/publications/reports/nanoscience-and-nanotechnologies-opportunities
Rudebeck, Clare (2005, 5 April). Fertility tourists: Last week, anonymous egg and sperm donation ended in Britain. *The Independent*.
Salter, Brian (2007). Bioethics, biopolitics and the moral economy of human embryonic stem cell science: The case of the European Union 6th Framework Programme. *New Genetics and Society*, 26(3), 269–88.
Sanchini, Virginia (2015). Bioethical expertise: Mapping the field. *Biblioteca della libertà*. www.centroeinaudi.it/images/abook_file/213_online_Sanchini.pdf
Schneiker, Andrea and Jutta Joachim (2018). Revisiting global governance in multistakeholder initiatives: Club governance based on ideational prealignments, *Global Society*, 32(1), 2–22.
Schön, Donald A. and Martin Rein (1994). *Frame Reflection: Toward the Resolution of Intractable Policy Controversies*, New York: Basic Books.
Schrefler, Lorna (2010). The usage of scientific knowledge by independent regulatory agencies. *Governance*, 23(2), 309–30.
Scientific Committee on Emerging and Newly Identified Health Risks (SCENIHR) (2007). Opinion on the Appropriateness of the Risk Assessment Methodology in Accordance with the Technical Guidance Documents for New and Existing Substances for Assessing the Risks of Nanomaterials. http://ec.europa.eu/health/ph_risk/committees/04_scenihr/docs/scenihr_o_010.pdf
Scott, James C. (1998). *Seeing Like a State: How Certain Schemes to Improve the Human Condition Have Failed*, New Haven: Yale University Press.
Seabrooke, Leonard and Lasse Folke Henriksen (eds.) (2017). *Professional Networks in Transnational Governance*, Cambridge: Cambridge University Press.
Seabrooke, Leonard and Eleni Tsingou (2009). Revolving Doors and Linked Ecologies in the World Economy: Policy Locations and the Practice of International Financial Reform, CSGR Working Paper No. 260/09, Coventry: Centre for the Study of Globalisation and Regionalisation.
Seabrooke, Leonard and Duncan Wigan (2016). Powering ideas through expertise:
Seligmann, Jean (1976, 12 April). A right to die, *Newsweek*.

Sending, Ole J. (2015). *The Politics of Expertise: Competing for Authority in Global Governance*, Ann Arbor: University of Michigan Press.

Shapin, Steven and Simon Schaffer (1985). *Leviathan and the Air-Pump*, Princeton: Princeton University Press.

Shillito, John (1969). The organ donor's doctor: A new role for the neurosurgeon. *New England Journal of Medicine*, 281(19), 1071–2.

Singer, Peter (1991). On being silenced in Germany. *New York Review of Books*. www.nybooks.com/articles/archives/1991/aug/15/on-being-silenced-in-germany

Steven, Martin (2009). Religious lobbies in the European Union: From dominant church to faith-based organization. *Religion, State and Society*, 37(2), 181–91.

Stone, Deborah (2012). *Policy Paradox: The Art of Political Decision Making*, revised edition, New York: W. W. Norton.

Stone, Diane (2017). Partners to Diplomacy: Transnational Experts and Knowledge Transfer among Global Policy Programs. In Annabelle Littoz-Monnet, ed., *The Politics of Expertise in International Organizations*, London: Routledge, pp. 89–106.

Strom, Stephanie (2014, 30 May). Companies quietly apply biofuel tools to household products. *New York Times*.

'Surgical showbiz' (1968, 22 January). *The Nation*.

ten Have, Henk A. M. J. and Bert Gordijn (2014). *Handbook of Global Bioethics*, Dordrecht: Springer Netherlands.

'The transplanted heart' (1967, 15 December). *Time*.

Thomasma, David C. (2002). Early bioethics. *Cambridge Quarterly of Healthcare Ethics*, 11(4), 335–43.

Trépos, Jean-Yves (1996). *La Sociologie de L'expertise*, Paris: Presses Universitaires de France.

Tsingou, Eleni (2015). Club governance and the making of global financial rules. *Review of International Political Economy*, 22(2), 225–56.

'UK reacts to Google "right to be forgotten" ruling' (2014, 21 May). *BBC News*. www.bbc.co.uk/news/technology-27499601

'Unable to reach an agreement, ministers close debate on stem cells' (2003, 6 December). *European Report*.

United Nations Educational, Scientific and Cultural Organization (UNESCO) (2010). Assisting Bioethics Committees (ABC) Project, SHS/EST/ABC/03/REV.2.

United Press International (1982, 24 February). France's first test-tube baby – A healthy, seven pound, ... www.upi.com/Archives/1982/02/24/Frances-first-test-tube-baby-a-healthy-seven-pound/7909383374800

Verdun, Amy (1999). The role of the Delors Committee in the creation of EMU: An epistemic community? *Journal of European Public Policy*, 6(2), 308–28.

Wade, Nicholas (2010, 20 May). Researchers say they created a synthetic cell. *New York Times*.

Warnock, Mary (1985). *A Question of Life: The Warnock Report on Human Fertilisation and Embryology*, New York: Basil Blackwell.

Warnock, Mary (1988). A national ethics committee. *British Medical Journal*, 297(6664), 1626–7.

'We climbed Everest' (1968, 1 January). *Newsweek*.

Weiss, Carol H. (ed.) (1977). Research for policy's sake: The enlightenment function of social research. *Policy Analysis*, 3(4), 553–65.

Weiss, Carol H. (1979). *Using Social Research in Public Policy Making*, Lanham, MD: Lexington Books.

Weiss, Carol H. (1982). Policy research in the context of diffuse decision making. *Journal of Higher Education*, 53(6), 619–39.

Weiss, Carol H. and Michael J. Bucuvalas (1980). *Social Science Research and Decision Making*, New York: Columbia University Press.

Weltring, Klaus-Michael (2005). *Network of Excellence: Nano2Life.* http://ec.europa.eu/archives/european_group_ethics/archive/2005_2010/activities/docs/weltringnano2life20dec05_en.pdf

White House (2000). *National Nanotechnology Initiative: Leading to the Next Industrial Revolution.* Report by the Interagency Working Group on Nanoscience, Engineering and Technology. https://clintonwhitehouse4.archives.gov/media/pdf/nni.pdf

White House Office of the Press Secretary (2011). Remarks by the President in State of Union Address. https://obamawhitehouse.archives.gov/the-press-office/2011/01/25/remarks-president-state-union-address

Wikler, Daniel and Jeremiah Barondess (1993). Bioethics and anti-bioethics in light of Nazi medicine: What must we remember? *Kennedy Institute of Ethics Journal*, 3(1), 39–55.

Wilhelm, Ernst-Oliver (2020). A brief history of the General Data Protection Regulation. https://iapp.org/resources/article/a-brief-history-of-the-general-data-protection-regulation

Wilson, Duncan (2014). *The Making of British Bioethics*, Manchester: Manchester University Press.

World Health Organization (WHO) (2011). *Global Network of WHO Collaborating Centers for Bioethics: Annual Report 2010–11.* www.who.int/ethics/partnerships/WHO_CC_Annual_Report_2010-2011.pdf

Zehfuss, Maja (2018). *War and the Politics of Ethics*, Oxford: Oxford University Press.

Zito, Anthony R. (2001). Epistemic communities, collective entrepreneurship and European integration. *Journal of European Public Policy*, 8(4), 585–603.

Index

Abbott, Andrew, 29
Action Group on Erosion, Technology and Concentration (ETC Group), 86
agency, possibility of, 11, 21, 34, 131
Alzheimer Europe, 97
applied ethics, 5, 6, 51
   specialised academic programmes, 6, 51
artificial intelligence, 2
assisted reproductive technology (ART), 56

Barroso, José Manuel, 76, 82, 89, 108, 110, 114
Beecher, Henry, 42–3, 45
Belmont Report, 49–50, 54–5, *See also* bioethical expertise; principlism
BEPA. *See* Bureau of European Policy Advisors
Berg, Paul, 46
Best, Jacqueline, 30–1
big data, 105, 109–10, 118, 145
   commercial and social added value, 103
bioethical expertise
   authority of, 5–6, 8, 16–17, 23, 35, 37
   emergence of, 11, 16–17, 55, 124
   mobilisation of, 9, 79–81, 92–4, 99–100, 122–3
   moral authorities, 1, 3
   production of, 71, 83, 99, 123
   stabilisation of, 9, 17, 37
   utilitarian framework, 9, 35, 38, 124, *See also* pro-science and innovation narrative
bioethical framing, 42, 68, 95
biomedical research, 1, 16, 48, 124
biosecurity, 110

biotechnology, 18, 59, 64, 68–9, 98
boundaries, expansion of, 2, 17
Bureau of European Policy Advisors, 19, 71–2, 83, 93, 99, 114–15
bureaucratic organisations, 32, 34, *See also* international organisations
Busquin, Philippe, 73–5, 84

calibration
   by private actors, 131–2
   definition of, 23, 35, 132
   examples of, 13, 34–5, 123, 131–2
   in data protection and privacy policy, 117–19
   in human embryonic stem cell policy, 79
capture, phenomena of, 131
Care for Europe, 67
CCNE. *See Comité Consultatif National d'Ethique*
Central and East European Association of Bioethics (CEEAB), 61
civil society
   actions, 18, 66, 93, 104, 109, 117
   citizen panels, 29
   consensus conferences, 29
   representation in policy, 14, 36, 49, 72, 93, 97
Clean Production Action, 86
closed policy community, 37, 72, 74, 83, 87, 92
codified knowledge. *See* expert knowledge
Cohen, David K., 34
co-legitimation, 10–13, 22, 32, 132, *See also* co-production of knowledge
Comité Consultatif National d'Ethique, 56
Comment on Reproductive Ethics (CORE), 67

155

Commission of the Bishops'
    Conferences of the European
    Community (COMECE), 67
conflict
    containment, 20, 37, 83, 99, 109,
        122–3
    manoeuvring, 2, 20, 79–80, 122, 123
    pre-empting, 37, 89, 90, 93, 110
    taming, 17, 23, 70, 75, 114, 124
consumers, 7, 36, 55, 88, 97
controversial policy agendas, 8,
    60, 102
co-production of knowledge, 10–12,
    21–3, 27–8, 63
Council of Europe, 62
crossing points, 33, 71–2, 83, 99, 130,
    See also ideational alignment
    examples of, 130
cybersecurity, 110

data protection and privacy policy, 19,
    101, 104, 114
    Data Value Chain Unit, 103
    Digital Agenda, 101–3, 108–9, 121
    Hustinx, Peter, 111
    privacy impact assessment, 118
    Reding, Viviane, 101, 104, 106,
        111–14, 116
    right to be forgotten, 105, 112–13,
        119
debate, technicalisation of, 19, 65, 71,
    75, 83
democratisation of politics, 42
Demortain, David, 33, 131
depoliticisation, 122, 124, 127
destabilisation, moments of, 11–12, 22,
    27, 30, 41
DG CONNECT. *See* Directorate
    General for Communications
    Networks, Content and
    Technology
DG ENTR. *See* Directorate General for
    Enterprise and Industry
DG HOME. *See* Directorate General
    for Home and Migration Affairs
DG INFSO. *See* Directorate General for
    Information Society and Media
DG JUSTICE. *See* Directorate General
    Justice, Fundamental Rights and
    Citizenship

DG RESEARCH. *See* Directorate
    General for Research and
    Innovation
DG SANCO. *See* Directorate General
    for Health and Consumers
Digital Europe, 119
disciplinary voices, 5, 36
disruptive events, 11, 31, *See also*
    destabilisation, moments of
dissenting voices, 12, 15, 34, 37
DNA, 3, 17, 46, 138

ECJ. *See* European Court of Justice
economic competitiveness, 7, 68, 99,
    103
economists, 7, 29
EGE. *See* European Group on Ethics
entrepreneurial policymakers, 11, 30
environmental groups, 8, 127
epistemic authority, 36, 74, 83
epistemic communities, 25
ethics
    compartmentalisation of, 19, 83
    creep, 4, 19, 50, 94
    expertisation of, 20, 38
ethics advisory committees, 4, 6, *See
    also* European Group on Ethics
    as deliberative and democratic
        mechanisms, 4, 36, 37, 127
    claims to universal expertise, 6, 16,
        36, 124
    definition of, 5
    disciplinary diversity, 6, 36
ethics experts
    genealogy of, 17, 41, 47, 63, 125
EuropaBio, 68
European Commission
    Fifth Framework Programme, 72, 84
    Sixth Framework Programme, 64, 69
    Seventh Framework Programme, 64,
        76–7, 78–9, 114, 116
    Directorate General for
        Communications, Networks,
        Content and Technology, 101,
        103–4, 108–9, 117, 121
    Directorate General for Enterprise
        and Industry, 72, 84, 88, 105,
        108–9, 117, 121
    Directorate General for Health and
        Consumers, 72, 84, 88, 96

Index

Directorate General for Home and Migration Affairs, 104, 106, 117
Directorate General for Information Society and Media, 104
Directorate General for Research and Innovation, 67, 70, 72, 78, 88, 101, 114–15
Directorate General Justice, Fundamental Rights and Citizenship, 102, 104–5, 112, 114, 121
European Research Advisory Board (ERAB), 68
Group of Advisers on the Ethical Implications of Biotechnology (GAEIB), 62
Scientific Committee on Emerging and Newly Identified Health Risks (SCENIHR), 88
European Court of Justice, 66
Oliver Brüstel v. *Greenpeace*, 66
European Data Protection Supervisor, 103, 112
European Federation of Neurological Associations (EFNA), 68
European Federation of Pharmaceutical Industries and Associations (EFPIA), 68
European Genetic Alliances' Network (EGAN), 68
European Group on Ethics
  as terrain of competition, 19, 101, 123
  creation and composition, 14
  Opinion 15, Ethical Aspects of Human Stem Cell Research, 70, 78
  Opinion 26, Ethics of Information and Communication Technologies, 112, 114–15
  Opinion 28, Ethics of Security and Surveillance Technologies, 114, 116, 118
  opinion on nanomedicine, 89, 95–6
  opinion on the ethical review of hESC FP7 research projects, 77, 78
European Parkinson's Disease Association (EPDA), 68
European Parliament, 69, 74, 79, 86, 98, 105

Committee on the Environment, Public Health, and Food Safety (ENVI), 98
European People's Party and European Democrats group (EPP-ED), 67
Green Party, 85–9, 99
European Platform for Patients' Organisations, Science and Industry (EPPOSI), 68
European Union General Data Protection Regulation, 120
evidence, transfer of, 12, 95, 99, 111, 115, 123, *See also* orchestration
existing frameworks, contestation of, 27, 30
experiments on human subjects, 70
expert bioethicists. *See* ethics experts
expert knowledge
  contestation, 132
  definition of, 5
  political uses of, 25–6
  production of, 17, 128
  'rationality project', 23–5
  scientific, 3–5, 51
expertise. *See* expert knowledge
experts
  presence in different policy domains, 15, 127
Eyal, Gil, 11, 30, 31

Facebook, 105–6, 107
France, 56–7
  bébé éprouvette, 56
  Comité National Consultatif d'Ethique, 56–7
  Mitterrand, François, 56–7
Friends of the Earth, 67, 87, 90, 125

gene editing, 2
genetic engineering, 40, 41, 46–7, 51, 67
genetically modified organisms, 8, 85–6, 109
genomics, 62, 69
Germany, 59–60, 67, 69, 74, 107
  Chancellor Schroeder, 60
  Merkel, Angela, 119
  National Ethikrat, 59

Germany (cont.)
  Nazism, memory of, 59–60
  Nuremberg Code, 42
global governance, 2, 4, 17, 24, 63, 128–31
  boundary spanners, 129
  clubs, 128–9
  exclusive character of, 128
  networks, 29–30, 93, 128–31
  revolving door phenomenon, 129
  transnational communities, 128–31
GMOs. *See* genetically modified organisms
Google, 105, 107, 111
governance
  empowering of certain actors, 28, 58
  informal mechanisms of, 2
  levels of, 11, 12, 17, 132
  modes of, 22, 27–9
  narratives, 6, 28–9, 30
  techniques, 28
governance arrangements, 27–8, 29–30, 32, *See also* governance, modes of
Greenpeace, 66–7, 69, 86, 87, 90, 93

Haas, Peter, 24–5
Hastings Center, 53, 55–6
  Hastings Center Report, 53
  Hastings Center Studies, 53
human cloning, 60, 67, 73
human dignity, 67, 78
human embryonic stem cell (hESC), 3, 18, 64
  Report on Human Embryonic Stem Cell Research, 74
human experimentation, 47, 52, 121
human life, instrumentalisation of, 70
human morality, 1

ideational alignment
  consensual policy narrative, 9, 20
  definition of, 23
  examples of, 13, 33, 123, 130–1
  in data protection and privacy policy, 111–12
  in human embryonic stem cell policy, 72, 80
  in nanotechnology policy, 83, 90, 96–8, 99

in vitro fertilisation (IVF), 56
industry, 29, 35, 87
  biotech, 7, 97
  chemical, 7
  pharmaceutical, 7, 85, 131
  telecom, 7, 119
Information and communication technologies (ICTs), 19, 101, 110–13
innovation race, 84
international organisations, 4, 25, 61–3
International relations (IR), 1–20, 23–5, 124, 128–9
iteration, logics of, 2, 9, 17, 22, 32, 123

Jasanoff, Sheila, 10, 31

Kaplan, Abraham, 24
Kennedy Institute of Ethics, 53, 55–6, 146, 151, 154
  BioethicsLine, 54
knowing, ways of, 12, 33, 128, 130
knowledge, forms of, 5, 16, 17, 28–9, 30, 32, 55, 124

Lasswell, Harold, 24
Latour, Bruno, 10, 26
legislative reform in data privacy, 19, 83, 110
Lindblom, Charles E., 34
lobbying strategies, 13, 68, 105–6, 120

mandated science. *See* regulatory science
matters of concern, 30
medical doctors, 5, 36
medicine, ethics of, 1, 17, 40, 50, *See also* ethics experts
modernity, 7–8
molecular biologists, 3, 5, 17, 36, 46
moral concepts, 5, 36, 53, 64
mutually reinforcing dynamic, 10

nanomedicine, 13, 18, 82–3, 91–3, 95–8
nanotechnology, 18, 82–7, 89–94, 122
  anticipatory and inclusive approach, 91, 93–4, 99

Index

Code of Conduct for Responsible Nanoscience and Nanotechnologies, 98
  ethical implications of, 18
  industrial applications, 82
  Nano2Life, 92, 97
  Nanosciences and Nanotechnologies: An Action Plan for Europe, 84, 87
  pro-science discourse in, 84, 95, 97, 99
  risks associated with, 82, 86, 88, 94
narratives
  alternative, 8, 11, 33, 37, 55
  counter, 32–3
  dominant, 7, 12, 32–3, 129, 131–2
  governance, 11, 22, 30
  scientific and technological, 44–7
National Ethics Committee Forum (NEC Forum), 115
neurologists, 5, 36
new industrial revolution. *See also* nanotechnology
NGOs. *See* non-governmental organisations
NIH. *See* National Institute of Health
Non-governmental organisations, 85–8, 125–8
  protests, 85, 90, 126
NSA. *See* US National Security Agency

OECD. *See* Organisation for Economic Cooperation and Development
ontological domain, 2, 16
orchestration
  by private actors, 12, 131
  definition of, 22, 32–3
  examples of, 12, 32, 123, 131
  in data protection and privacy policy, 110–11
  in human embryonic stem cell policy, 65, 72, 77–9, 80
  in nanotechnology policy, 83, 90, 95–6, 99
organ transplants, debates over, 44–6
Organisation for Economic Cooperation and Development, 7
oversight of scientists, 40, 45, 48, 56, 58

patent law, 18, 64, 66
patients, organisations of, 68

philosophers, 36–7, 59
pluralist democracies, 1, 4, 36
polarisation, 109, 117
policy compromises, fabric of, 2
policy conflict, 19, 64, 80, 83, 101, 122
policy process, meso-level of, 12, 21–3, 27
policy solutions, 11, 26, 38, 75, 128
policymaking, insulation of, 2, 37, 94, 122
political debates, 2, 9, 102, 124
political narratives, 27, *See also* narratives
politicisation
  of debates, 8, 75, 102, 121
  of expertise, 25, 125
precautionary principle, 86, 125
preimplantation genetic diagnosis (PGD), 59
principlism, 52, 55–6, 63, 124, *See also* Belmont Report
  Principles of Bioethics, 54
privacy and civil rights associations, 106, 108
private actors. *See* industry
problematisation, 30, 41
professional agendas, 2, 42
professional ecologies, 129
pro-life advocates, 60, 67, 68
proportionality, principle of, 70, 118, *See also* principlism
pro-science and innovation narrative, 6, 31, 69
  market-oriented framing, 35, 123
  pro-innovation bias, 7
  speed imperative, 7
public accountability, 3, 58
public authorities, 88, 103, 113
public opposition, 8
public policy, 21, 23, 47, 54, 148

rationalist framework. *See* utilitarian framework
reflexivity, 5, 36
Registration, Evaluation, Authorization and Restriction of Chemical Substances (REACH), 88–9
  inclusion of nanomaterials, 89
regulatory experts, 7
regulatory science, 14, 140

religious groups, 8, 65, 67
reproductive medicine, 3, 56
reprogenetic technologies, 59
resources, distribution of, 12
risk assessment, 29, 88, 96

science and technology studies (STS), 10, 21, 26
scientific activity, regulation of, 42, 48
scientific and technological innovation, 23, See also pro-science and innovation narrative
  contestation, 7–8, 31
  controversies, 3–4, 8, 37, 44, 47, 99
  ethical implications of, 5, 36
  governance of, 2, 3–4
  industry and commercialisation, 7, 125
  regulation of, 66, 85, 89, 101, 108, 125
scientific rationality, 5, 40
scientific self-government, 3, 11, 39
scientists, authority of, 3, 31
Seabrooke, Leonard, 129
security technologies, 108, 110, 114, 118, 121
Snowden crisis, 114, 116–17, 119
social practices, 10, 21
social scientists, 24, 52, 59, 125
sociotechnical imaginary, 6
special knowledge. See expert knowledge
specialists. See ethical experts
stabilisation, mechanisms of, 12, 32, 35, 63, 65, 130, See also orchestration, ideational alignment and calibration
state-science relations, 3
statisticians, 29
Stone, Diane, 26, 128
supranational arenas, 2
surveillance, 103–4, 108, 110, 114–16, 118–19
sustainable growth, 7, 102
synthetic biology, 2, 20, 125–7, 146
  biofuels, production of, 126

technical advisors, 8, See also ethics experts
Terrorist Finance Tracking Programme, 105
theologians, 5, 13, 35–7, 40–1, 48, 50
think tanks, 33
Tsingou, Eleni, 129, 131

UK. See United Kingdom, the
uncertainty in policy, 25, 100
UNESCO. See United Nations Educational, Scientific and Cultural Organisation
United Kingdom, the, 56–9, 85
  British Medical Association, 57
  Centre for Medical Law and Ethics at Kings College, 58
  Commissioner, 107
  Kennedy, Ian, 58
  Nuffield Foundation, 59
  Royal Society, the, 85
  Warnock Commission, 58
  Warnock, Mary, 58
United Nations Convention on Biological Diversity, 126
United Nations Educational, Scientific and Cultural Organisation, 61–3
  Division on Ethics of Science and Technology, 62
  International Bioethics Committee (IBC), 62
United States, the, 105–7, 116, 125–6
  civil rights movement, 45
  Institutional Review Boards (IRBs)
  Kennedy, Edward, 47, 48, 53
  Krugman, Saul, 42
  National Commission for the Protection of Human Subjects of Biomedical and Behavioural Research, 48–50, 54–5
  National Institutes of Health, 49
  Obama, Barack, 125–7
  Presidential Commission for the Study of Bioethical Issues (PCSBI), 125
  Rockefeller Foundation, 53, 54
  Tuskegee experiment, 43–4, 48

Index

US Department of Commerce, 106
US Department of Health and Human Services, 43
US Federal Trade Commission, 105–7
US National Security Agency, 116
Willowbrook facility, 42–4
US. *See* United States, the

Weiss, Carol, 24–5
workable policy scenario, 8, 34, 65, 71, 102
World Health Organisation, 62
  Global Network of Experts, 62
  Global Summit of National Bioethics Advisory Bodies, 62
Wikler, Daniel, 62

Zehfuss, Maja, 124

CPSIA information can be obtained
at www.ICGtesting.com
Printed in the USA
LVHW021220030821
694401LV00003B/271